The Faith Factor

Unlocking God's
Amazing Plan
For Your Abundant Life

by

F. Chapin Marsh, III, Ed.D.

Black Forest Press
San Diego, California
May, 2004
First Edition

The Faith Factor

Unlocking God's Amazing Plan For Your Abundant Life

by

F. Chapin Marsh, III, Ed.D.

Printed in the United States of America
by
Black Forest Press
PO Box 6342
Chula Vista, CA 91909-6342

Contracts, Administration and Inquiries
(800) 451-9404
Marketing, Sales and Promotions
(888) 808-5440

Permission

Verses marked NKJV are taken from The New King James Version, copyright 1979 and 1982 by Thomas Nelson, Inc. Publishers. Used by perrmission.

Disclaimer

This document is an original work of the author. It may include reference to information commonly known or freely available to the general public. Any resemblance to other published information is purely coincidental. The author has in no way attempted to use material not of his own origination. Black Forest Press disclaims any association with or responsibility for the ideas, opinions or facts as expressed by the author of this book.

Printed in the United States of America
Library of Congress
Cataloging-in-Publication

ISBN: 1-58275-046-7

TABLE OF CONTENTS

What They're Saying vii

Dedication ix

Acknowledgements x

Author's Note xi

Publisher's Note xiii

Foreword xv

Prologue xvii

Faith Factor One: A Shot in the Dark: 1
    Three Layers of Faith

Faith Factor Two: God Has Great Things Planned For You: 15
    Three Definitions of Faith

Faith Factor Three: Faith and Knowing God's Will: 31
    Three Stages of Faith

Faith Factor Four: A.S.K.: Three Keys to Faith 43

Faith Factor Five: God Will Lift You Up: 53
    Three Voices of Faith

Faith Factor Six: The WOW Factor!: Three Cycles of Faith ... 63

Faith Factor Seven: The Enemy Within: 75
    Three Enemies of Faith

Faith Factor Eight: The Upside Down Life: 91
    Three Opportunities for Faith

Faith Factor Nine: A Gift Unopened: 107
    Three Outcomes of Faith

Faith Factor Ten: Dream Big: 121
    Three Mystical Truths of Faith.

Epilogue 137

Dr. F. Chapin Marsh, III

WHAT THEY'RE SAYING

The best book I have read regarding faith.
-Dr. Richard Andujo
Headmaster, The Rock Academy

The Faith Factor *is a breath of fresh air revitalizing the soul with a reminder of God's awesome promises.*
-Roger Vaus
President, Youth Development, Inc.

We all struggle, we all falter, but The Faith Factor *works on my soul, not just my mind. I would recommend this book to anyone looking to take action in their spiritual life.*
-Buddy Cummings
President/CEO, Media All Stars

Dr. Marsh skillfully uses human and family stories to illustrate God's loving attributes. In his informal and eminently readable style, he makes profound spiritual truth easy to grasp and understand . . . I enjoyed the book and think it is an excellent primer on faith issues. As I have mentioned, the examples and stories from real life used were great.
-Jeff Badger, Esq.
Long and Badger, Salisbury, MD

Excellent, Excellent, Excellent! This is a great God inspired piece of work. I believe everyone should read it!
I give a full recommendation and endorsement to this piece of work. As I read through the chapters, the book spoke directly to me. At times, it brought me to tears, and other times, I laughed out loud, but most of all, it's an excellent teaching tool. As an Educational Administrator and Professor for over 25 years, I learned greatly. I believe everyone should read this book.
-Dr. Wes Forbes
Alliant University

The descriptive writing by the author provides such a clear, vivid picture that I found myself drawn into the scene being described as if I was there. The story in each chapter provides analogies that really drove home the message that parallels God's work and direction He has given us. The message in this book that Dr. Marsh provides has made me challenge my faith and rethink some of the decisions I made for me in life. This is a "must read" for everyone—Christian and non-Christian alike. . .

-Dr. Wes Forbes
Alliant University

I just got through reading your book and really enjoyed your faith story. It was very relevant timing as we step out in faith and start our ministry. I was extremely moved the story about Cade and his $10. It's amazing how much our kids can teach us. Thanks for sharing with me. I'm looking forward to your second book.

-Steve Adkins
Campus Crusade for Christ
Salisbury, Maryland

I have seen my faith steadily increase ever since I started reading and applying the concepts in The Faith Factor. *It provides me with a fresh perspective on how to look at faith in my life. In the past, I have tended to over-mystify the concept, but* The Faith Factor *broke it down into its core components, and the action items in each chapter gave me clear steps on how to incrementally increase my faith.*

-Joel Davies
COO, Principal, Media All Stars

Make sure that any Biblical leader you know gets a copy right now! I put this book on a list of Bridge's Pursuit of Holiness *and Lewis'* Mere Chrisianity. Faith Factor *is a must have book!*

-Howard Everett
Pastor, Calvary Baptist Church

DEDICATION

This book is dedicated to my visionary father,
Papa Freddie.
He finally got it right:

1. Follow Jesus every day the best you can.

2. Everything else will take care of itself.

3. Repeat.

Thanks, Dad! I love you!

ACKNOWLEDGEMENTS

Jesus, thank you! Additionally I want to thank my wonderful wife, Christine, for her prayful support. Cade, Cana and Cally, I love you. Thanks to Jennie Nelson, Judy Corbin, Brent Cole, Wes Anderson, and Jeff Badger for editing support.

I am grateful to Mike MacIntosh who has always been an encouragement to me. I have prayed this book would bless and encourage many. To those who purchase and pass this book along, thank you.

In His Mighty Grip,

F. Chapin Marsh III, Ed.D
San Diego, California

AUTHOR'S NOTE

The Faith Factor: Unlocking God's Amazing Plan for Your Abundant Life is nothing more than one man's take on this wonderful, quirky, exciting, and hopeful journey called the Christian life. The purpose of this book is twofold. First, it is designed to be "loaned" from friend to friend, Christian or not, so that anyone "exploring" Christianity or desiring to understand the deeper things of faith in Christ may do so in a composed and thoughtful manner. Second, it is hoped the Christian reader will be exhorted or spurred on to fulfill the great works God has in store for every one of us as we take Him at His Word and live our lives by faith.

The Faith Factor is written in an unconventional way. It was not written as a sanitized book on Christian doctrine. Quite frankly, it doesn't even scratch the surface of faith. My hope is that people, real people with real needs, fears, hopes, and disappointments will read this book and be encouraged as well as challenged. I pray that lonely, unfulfilled people the world over will stop living confusing lives of miserable convenience. I pray that executives and pastors, homemakers and high-schoolers, presidents and college students will read this book and have their lives changed for good, forever in Christ by faith.

The Faith Factor is written to encourage you to live your life by faith. The *Faith Factor* is written in 10 simple, easy-to-read chapters. *The Faith Factor* ends each chapter with a recap of the specific FACTOR of FAITH shared in that chapter, as well as an action item for that chapter. *The Faith Factor* can be read alone or in a small group or Bible study.

The Faith Factor is what separates Christians from non-Christians. It is the dividing line between heaven and hell. It is the key to the door of purpose and hope. Without the key of faith one might endure a life of emptiness, futility, and frustration. The reason is simple: faith unlocks God's amazing plan for a Christian's abundant life. *The Faith Factor* changes people's lives for the better. *The Faith Factor* can change your life for the better. *The Faith Factor* has changed my life for the better, well beyond anything I could have ever dreamt of. That's why I wrote this book for you. Enjoy!

The Faith Factor: Unlocking God's Amazing Plan for Your Abundant Life is volume one. If you have stories of faith, please write us or e-mail us with your story. You may find God using your life in our next volume to minister and witness to many people who just might need to hear what God has done through your life of faith. The true secret, if there is one regarding faith, is this: Biblical faith is effortless and wonder-filled since real faith is simply listening to God, obeying God, then enjoying God using our surrendered lives to fulfill His plan for us and the generation in which we live.

Faith is something that grows with heavy doses of application. The more we read the Bible, share our faith experiences, and listen to others living by faith, the more apt you and I are to begin living by faith in our lives. Faith is like a muscle. The more you use it the more it grows. The less you use it the less it grows. It is a little like use it or lose it.

Writing down in a spiritual journal the things God is doing in your life by faith makes for encouragement today. It can help you see progress in your life as well as God's faithfulness. It also provides insight for future generations into your life, the times you lived, God's faithfulness, and intimate and relevant examples of how to live a life of faith, to honor God and share the Gospel of Jesus Christ. In essence, you could say that as you and I journal, we are actually recording the fifth Gospel. It is the Gospel of our lives. It is time to live by faith. I hope this book helps.

PUBLISHER'S NOTE

For every 100 or so books which Black Forest Press publishes, one particular book, such as The Faith Factor by Dr. F. Chapin Marsh III, stands out among the rest. It is not that the book itself will be more competitive in the marketplace, or that it will challenge its contemporary counterparts in the book world for high sales, but for the simple reason that it contains those hard to find golden nuggets of spiritual wisdom and guidance that every human being needs to hear and be aware of on a daily basis.

Having scholastic value and literary worth is one thing, but providing a reader with discerning rhetoric that penetrates their minds and hearts and causes action and reflection on their part, is very powerful. The Faith Factor does just that! How many of us think we know about faith, yet treat faith as some fleeting feathery notion, or with light-hearted thinking rather than using this gift, as a tool of incomparable magnitude. Faith displayed is a means of not only influencing others by our proven convictions but it becomes an intensely effective example of one's strong personal confidence that faith actually works. Our faith is a living faith; it tells God, through our obedience, that we are humbling ourselves by succumbing to His perfect will. We do this by professing how we need Him and trust Him without any hesitation, reservation or second thought. Ask, seek and knock! Call on His name!

Dr. Marsh has provided the reader with three keys to better understand and demonstrate faith. Ask! Seek! and Knock! He points out that we must obey God fully so we may be blessed. . .and reap the fruit of an obedient life. Let The Faith Factor unlock the Lord's amazing plan for the abundant life you deserve. Have faith, demonstrate it and use it daily with prayer. Keep this book in your own pile of very special books that you refer to often because I believe you will.

It is always an extreme pleasure to endorse such books as The Faith Factor. Like Dr. Wes Forbes of Alliant University says, "This is a must read!"

Dahk Knox, Ph.D., Ed.D.

CEO/Publisher

Black Forest Press

FOREWORD

Chapin Marsh has always had a heart for Jesus since he first became a Christian. *The Faith Factor* is a reflection of that love that is expressed from the servant to the Master. The reader is encouraged to be a person of faith, and to walk by faith and not by sight.

Working with children can be very challenging to anyone that does not *have* faith. Faith has a certain indefinable amount of flexibility to it; and this is the faith that Chapin Marsh learned as a young man—that he would trust in God to oversee the high school while he did the menial chores, and was the head cheerleader for the next generation.

I recommend this book, *The Faith Factor,* to all, and encourage you to question the enthusiasm of your faith. *The Faith Factor* will challenge you to grow day by day in this fascinating arena that God has designed for His people to live in.

Mike MacIntosh
Senior Pastor
Horizon Christian Fellowship
San Diego, California

PROLOGUE

*What if...in writing a spiritual journal the audience was set on a treasure hunt? What if...in including personal and poignant illustrations from one's lifetime the audience was pointed to a heavenly inheritance? What if...that audience two generations henceforth understood that "A good man leaves an inheritance to his children's children...." **Proverbs 13:22**. What if...this spiritual journal was that treasure, inheritance, personal love letter for a future generation. What if...it were a spiritual time capsule discovered like the treasure of El Dorado. What if...*

A young woman found her grandfather's spiritual journal. She might read the first journal in a twelve-volume set she discovered so far. The young lady may have settled Indian style in a dusty, mothball-scented attic with rays of light streaming through two broken holes in the upper left windowpane. The dust was thick, acrid, and visible, even as she breathed it through the crust-caked roof of her mouth. The paint on the window long ago chipped and standing like a bow legged sentinel. Her knee cut by a rusty nail bent out of position as she moved her body to get better light to read...while the light gradually slipped into gray.

Perhaps as she closed the bent cedar chest lock and had it crumble in her hands, she would wander between a mystical intensity and spooky sublimity. In reading his journal, she would notice her grandfather began each chapter "Beloved" and ended each chapter "Agape Papa." To the young lady it was as if he intended his journal to be read by someone who knew and loved him. Straight

*away she noticed her grandfather lived an adventurous and super-
natural life. She became intrigued to learn more about his life.
This first journal seemed to focus exclusively on faith. It began in
a compelling fashion...*

Beloved,

Today I resigned my position as Executive Pastor at a large non-
denominational church of over 4,000 people. I have no offer for
another position. I have no prospects. I have been journaling on
faith for over a year, so I assume I am close to "unlocking God's
amazing plan for my abundant life." I have a family of five, no job,
no prospects and a journal that now seems to be a provocative illustration on faith.

Interestingly, in my daily devotional readings today I read the following from *A Day's Journey* by Jon Courson.

*"By faith Abraham, when he was called to go out into a place
which he should after receive for an inheritance, obeyed;
and he went out, not knowing whither he went."* **Hebrews 11:8**

Abraham didn't know where he was going—he just started moving.
Most of us in his position would say, "Father, I know You're calling me to leave Ur, and I'll be happy to go as soon as you give me
a map of Mesopotamia."

But the Lord doesn't work that way in the arena of faith. *"Start
moving one step at a time,"* He says. *"I'll direct you, but I will not
give you directions for step two until you first take step one."* A
step of faith is a prerequisite for a man or woman to be used by
God. God is looking for those who will come to the Jordan and get
their feet wet. *Joshua 3:15*

My natural tendency, however, is to say, *"Here I am, Lord. Right near the edge, just like You told me to be. Now, Lord, this ark is important cargo. You don't want to see it get dropped in the river and carried downstream, do you? That's not practical. So in order to help you protect your good name, whenever you part the water, I'll be thrilled to go across. Here I am, Your man of faith, ready to serve you on the spot."* That is human nature, not faith.

Without faith it is impossible to please God. *"Why?"* You ask. *"Why does God take me to the edge of the Jordan, tell me to put my foot in, and risk me looking like a fool or the ark floating down the river? I don't get it."*

Guess what? You will get it—because faith is the *lingua franca* of eternity. God is not saying, *"I am going to put you to the test for the fun of it. Let's see if you step in or not."* The father has no joy seeing his kids agonize at the edge of the Jordan. *"If this causes you agony,"* He says, *"it is because you yet need to become a man of faith. After all, it is who you are in the arena of faith that will affect how I will use you in the next billion years to come."*

You see, gang, if you take eternity out of the equation, the whole thing seems like a bad joke. But once you understand that this whole deal on earth is to train, stretch, develop and mature you for heaven and the ages to come, then you will start looking at everything in that way. *"OK father,"* you'll say; *"this is a stretch for me. It is uncomfortable. It is not easy. But You told me to be like Abraham, so even if I don't know where I'm going, I trust You"*

Agape Papa

The young lady again noticed it seemed that her grandfather was writing his spiritual journal for someone to read in the future. In fact so much of what he wrote spoke to her both personally and spiritually. Since she was at this point in her life, thirsty for spiritual truth and insight, she eagerly anticipated the next chapter in her grandfather's journal. There would be many questions to be pondered as she read. For example on the cover of his spiritual journal, her grandfather had inscribed the following:

"A good man leaves an inheritance to his children's children..." **Proverbs 13:22**

She reached over an old ripped box of dirty clothes, snapped a rough-hewn black light switch that made a loud "click." The light bulb flickered through a maze of brittle cobwebs. "Pop!" The light bulb burst into a thousand shards...just like her life....

FAITH FACTOR ONE

A Shot in the Dark: Three Layers of Faith

THE FALL

Beloved,

I fell down again today. It was my third or fourth fall, today. I feel pretty good though. It's still morning.

Perhaps you have felt like I feel. I want to "do the right thing." I try to "be all I can be." I have just one problem: I keep "missing the mark."

I have spent enormous time, energy, and money attempting to "uncover my unlimited potential." I have inhaled self-help books like a first grader eating candy on Halloween. I have attended intensive "life-changing" seminars and listened to self-proclaimed gurus tell me their secrets to unlocking "unlimited wealth," my "power potential," "dynamic dieting," and worse. Nothing ever lasted. Nothing.

So, though I try, I fell down today, again. Hey, I set goals; for example, I wake up daily. I shower and dress myself, which is asking an awful lot some days. I have lived a decent life. I have no criminal record and wonder how that happened. I have always wondered about the meaning of life, and how I fit in.

Life is about following directions. I am learning to follow directions, for which my mother will be grateful. Life is full of directions. Directions lead to life and, when not followed, sometimes to death. Consider for a moment: you are on your roof and you decide to jump. Gravity (life's direction that stuff falls to earth from tall buildings) comes into play and begins to work in your life whether or not you believe in gravity (and whether or not you believe the directions that explain gravity and its consequences). The consequences of ignoring those directions are obvious: what you fall on and land on will determine whether you live or die.

Today, I fell down again, which for me is trying but failing to do what I know is the right thing. I chose not to follow the instructions that directly affected my life. Most people know what to do; they simply choose not to do it. They sort of throw the directions out with the trash. Things like diets, exercise, consumption issues, kindness and forgiveness of others, making a hard phone call, writing a book, and committing to a life of faith all require a choice to follow directions. Today, I fell down again.

DIRECTIONS

Sometimes the directions for life are right in front of us. I have found that when I think I am familiar with something, the less inclined I am to follow the directions. In putting together a bike, for example, failure to follow directions can be dangerous. In life not following directions from the Bible can be eternally damning. *"Not everyone who says to Me, 'Lord, Lord,' shall enter the kingdom of heaven, but he who does the will of My Father in heaven. Many will say to Me in that day, 'Lord, Lord have we not prophesied in Your name, cast out demons in Your name, and done many wonders in Your name?' And then I will declare to them, 'I never knew you; depart from Me, you who practice lawlessness.'"*

Matthew 7:21-23

The directions for life are found quite conveniently in the Bible. Someone told me the BIBLE was God's Basic Instructions Before Leaving Earth—*Bible*. Someone even older noted it was God's love letters to you and me. The Bible is alive with truth for living.

DOING FINE...I THINK

Someone very close to me shared the following story that I believe speaks to the idea that though we think we are doing fine, we in fact, are not. Worse yet, the day is fast approaching when our misguided sense of ourselves will be exposed and great hurt may come our way. In everyday life it can be traumatic. In the eternal scheme of things it will be devastating. Here is his story.

Recently, I had a very good friend forget about me. There was a party of sorts and many friends and acquaintances of mine were invited. It was an event celebrating something my family and I had dearly invested our lives in. It was an event my friend forgot to invite me to.

At first I chose to assume the best. I believed he had simply mailed the invitation to our last residence. Since we moved, I thought we had missed the invitation in the mail. I called him to find out how the affair went and soon discovered our invitation had probably not been lost in the mail. It soon became apparent that we had not been invited to the festivities.

To say our disappointment was deep is to understate the emotion of the snub. I had served and loved so many of the people at the celebration. Surely, they had felt the same for us. How well intentioned and horribly wrong I was. In considering the depth of our relationship with these people I had overestimated my importance.

This incident made me consider how it will feel for those of us who are seemingly dedicated to serving Jesus when He says to us, "I never knew you." Despair! Disbelief! Disappointment! In the end, my friends' family was hurt, a little angry, and had to fight off bitterness. But the results of being overlooked eternally will be devastating. At the end of all our lives, how we choose to follow or ignore God's directions from the Bible will determine if we will know peace or have no peace.

It seems everything in life has a set of directions. Faith it turns out can be understood from its own set of directions. This is good. Faith has three essential layers.

JOURNEY TO FAITH

These layers begin with our **philosophy of life** or our **journey to faith**. People are either Atheist (don't believe in God), or Agnostic (ignorant about God), or Theist (believe in a form of God). Like most people, I have embraced all three at one point or another. All people believe in something, and what they believe affects how they live.

COMMITMENT TO FAITH

The second layer of faith is **whom we choose to follow**. It is our commitment to faith. In my atheistic days, I found atheists follow their own inclinations and the end result is a form of anarchy and hedonism. Agnostics and some theists spend their lives on a futile journey following a series of wrong men, ideas, or causes. In my life, secular humanism and a kind of blended form of psychology and capitalism became my gods. I noted that most of modern faith comes down to this:

Buddha—DEAD
Confucius—DEAD
Mohammed—DEAD
L. Ron Hubbard—DEAD
Joseph Smith—DEAD
Skinner, Jung, Freud, Leary—DEAD
Darwin, Marx, Lenin, Mao—DEAD
Jesus Christ—died, raised from the dead—**alive!**

LIFE OF FAITH

The third layer of faith deals with **how we purpose to live our lives**. This is our life by faith. We will spend most of our time discussing this third layer of faith. This third layer of faith begins after you make a commitment to a philosophy of life (journey to faith), and a commitment to the person you will follow (commitment of faith), and then decide how you purpose to live your life (life of faith begins). The passion and purpose with which you live your life has meaningful and eternal consequences as this following story exhibits.

A teenager lived alone with his father, and the two of them had a very special relationship. Even though the son was always on the bench, his father was always in the stands cheering. He never missed a game. This young man was still the smallest in his class when he entered high school. His father continued to encourage the son but also made it very clear that he did not have to play football if he didn't want to.

The young man loved football and decided to hang in there. He was determined to try his best at every practice, and perhaps he'd get a chance to play when he was a senior.

All through high school he never missed a practice or a game, but remained a bench warmer all four years. His faithful father was always in the stands, always with words of encouragement for him.

When the young man went to college, he decided to try out for the football team as a "walk-on." Everyone was sure he could never make the cut, but he did. The coach admitted that he kept the boy on the roster because he always put his heart and soul into every practice, and at the same time exemplified for the other members the spirit and hustle they badly needed.

The news that he had survived the cut thrilled him so much that he rushed to the nearest phone and called his father. His father shared his excitement and was sent season tickets for the college games.

This persistent young athlete never missed practice during his four years at college, but he never got to play in the game.

It was the end of his senior football season, and as he trotted out onto the practice field shortly before the big playoff game, the coach met him with a telegram. The young man read the telegram and he became deathly silent.

Swallowing hard, he mumbled to the coach, "My father died this morning. Is it all right if I miss practice today?" The coach put his arm gently around his shoulder and said, "Take the rest of the week off, son. And don't even plan to come back to the game on Saturday."

Saturday arrived, and the game was not going well. In the third quarter, when the team was ten points behind, a silent young man quietly slipped into the empty locker room and put on his football gear. As he ran onto the sidelines, the coach and his players were astounded to see their faithful teammate back so soon.

"Coach, please let me play. I've just got to play today," said the young man. The coach pretended not to hear him. There was no way he wanted his worst football player in this close playoff game. But the young man persisted, and finally, feeling sorry for the kid, the coach gave in. "All right," he said. "You can go in."

Before long the coach, players and everyone in the stands could not believe their eyes. This little unknown, who had never played before, was doing everything right. The opposing team could not stop him. He recovered an on-side kick, blocked like a rhino protecting its young, picked up a fumble for a touchdown, and tackled as if the ball carrier were running away with the young man's every possession. His team began to triumph.

The score was soon tied. In the closing seconds of the game, this kid intercepted a pass and ran all the way for the winning touchdown. The fans broke loose. His teammates hoisted him onto their shoulders. Such cheering you've never heard!

Finally, after the stands had emptied and the team had showered and left the locker room, the coach noticed that the young man was sitting quietly in the corner all alone. The coach came to him and said, "Kid, I can't believe it. You were fantastic! Tell me what got into you? How did you do it?"

The young man looked at the coach, with tears in his eyes, and said, "Well you knew my dad died, but did you know my dad was blind?" The young man swallowed hard and forced a smile.

*"Dad came to all my games, but today was
the first time he could see me play, and I wanted to
show him I could do it."*

Author Unknown

It may be a great help for those like me who thought they had made a commitment yet perhaps did not fully follow through on the directions. I know that at times in my life I needed help even figuring out where the directions were located. It helped me to know others struggled through life, seemingly "put together" yet still longing for hope and meaning in their lives. It was reading or hearing stories or "testimonies" that helped me see my own need for help.

I realized eventually that I needed to stop ignoring these stories or testimonies of people's lives. I realized that many people were like me; they needed hope but often were afraid or too tired to ask. I found a beautiful example of a testimony from my pastor. I have shared this with many people. I would like to share it now with you. I hope it helps clear away some doubts for you or someone you love. If it speaks to you, perhaps you can share it with someone you care for too.

A SHOT IN THE DARK

Enjoy this story; it will change your life.

Rammm...

Michael Kirk MacIntosh modulated his voice as the guru had taught him, chanting the sacred word slowly, letting its sound reverberate across the desert floor while he sat and stared at the ghostly outlines of Yucca Valley. Ram...ramm...rammm...

It was four o'clock in the morning, and Michael was hallucinating. The LSD had taken hold, and cosmic music was flooding his brain. He was waiting for a flying saucer to appear.

Michael MacIntosh had seen and done it all: marriage on a whim that lasted six weeks; UFO-watching in a drug-induced haze; incarceration in a mental ward of the Orange County Medical Center. He was a free spirit, a product of the 60's...but he couldn't have been more miserable.

Michael was born to a working-class family in Portland, Oregon, March 26, 1944. His father was a handsome man who went into electronics, but a taste for drink and a lust for gambling made him considerably less than a perfect husband, or father. As for Michael's mother, all her life she has known struggle. Yet throughout her three troubled marriages she was able to bequeath one priceless gift to Michael and his two older brothers: a sense of humor.

From this rough and troubled beginning, young Michael entered his adult world with less than a full set of useful tools. And when life hit him full force, he hadn't a clue how to respond. In 1959, Michael's brother David, the "star" in his life, was killed in an automobile accident, and Michael's life was turned upside down. Grief and depression led him to begin an eleven-year spiral downward, a ride filled with alcohol, drugs, lies, gangs and women.

Through the 60's Michael saw himself as a fun-loving, happy-go-lucky, joke-telling, woman-chasing, beer-drinking, average guy. But inside he was a completely different person: lonely, empty, insecure, with no self-confidence or self-esteem, completely void of purpose or direction. He eventually moved to Southern California and became a full-time member of the beach crowd.

The outgoing, bronzed panhandler was invited to a party one evening, where he met an attractive young college student named Sandy. They talked all night; Michael became infatuated; and four weeks later they were married, barefoot in Las Vegas. Two or three months of excitement followed, but actually the marriage went badly from the beginning. Although he truly loved her, Michael's doubts and fears would overwhelm the responsibilities of family life.

After three years of an up-and-down marriage and the birth of two wonderful children, Michael's drug-induced fantasies took their toll. When he told Sandy's brother he was working for the CIA on a flying saucer project, the family finally admitted, 'Mike's just **completely gone!**' The lifestyle he had chosen had destroyed his mind and, Sandy felt, their relationship along with it.

HITTING BOTTOM

Michael was definitely on his way down, and hit bottom three weeks later in the rundown shack of a drug pusher and Satan worshiper named Ron. After swallowing a capsule of LSD laced with strychnine, Michael began to lose touch with reality. His vision blurred and his speech became tangled. The prospect of a violent death engulfed him, and he imagined Ron was a hit man assigned by the Mafia to murder him.

Then Michael passed out and dreamt that several of Ron's followers tied him up, put a bag over his head and robbed him. Finally awakening and sitting in the darkness, he 'saw' spirit forms hovering around him, including the guru Maharishi, Krishna and the Buddha himself. He called to them 'Help me. I'm not ready to die! Please get me to God!' They mocked him and cackled their reply, 'This is as far as we take man!'

Thinking the bag was still over his head, Michael bumped his way into a bedroom. He knelt down and tried to pray, then imagined something go up against the side of his head. He pictured Ron and his revolver.

BANG! There was a sudden explosion! In his mind's eye Michael saw a huge fireball with flames shooting up into a mushroom cloud. He thought he ought to tell people to turn to God before it was too late. He dared not touch his head, though, because he was certain there was a huge cavity there and half his brain had been shot away.

Convinced his brain had exploded, Michael turned himself in to the police, who carefully took him to the mental health unit at Orange County Medical Center hospital. In reality, Michael was NOT shot that day, but the physical and psychological effects of that drug trip would haunt him for years.

NEW LIFE

After seventeen months of psychological therapy, Michael was ready to try life again, though he still felt mentally crippled from the devastation of drug abuse, and he kept reliving the horror of feeling he was shot. He moved in with his brother, Kent, and soon entered college, where he made a momentous discovery…he met some Christians.

It never occurred to Michael that young people would carry their Bibles to college. Their looks troubled him, for they had long hair and looked like hippies, but he had to admit they were happy and full of love. In all his involvement in the drug culture at the rock concerts and elsewhere, he had never seen the peace and happiness that these men and women seemed to have. And when he talked to them about it, they credited it all to Jesus Christ.

It was not long after that that one of Michael's classmates invited him to a concert at a nearby church, Calvary Chapel. Michael had heard the group sing before, so he decided he wouldn't mind hearing them again. When he arrived at the church, he was not prepared for what awaited him. The sanctuary, designed for 350 people, was jammed with over one thousand, and what was most amazing, they were all young and casually dressed.

'Something's wrong here,' he thought. *'Church people don't look like this. Where are the suits, the robes, the hymnbooks? They're not embarrassed to be here, and they're not embarrassed about Jesus!'*

When the young preacher, a former hippie himself, finished the message, he extended a gospel invitation. "Is there anybody here tonight who has left God? Perhaps you knew him as a youth, and now would like to know Him personally?" Michael's heart was struck and pierced as he remembered a commitment he had made as a child and realized he was the one the pastor was talking about. He stood up.

The wandering star came back into orbit. The freaked-out flower child was about to turn into a servant of the Most High. Michael knew his moment of decision had come. He was forever changed.

FAST FORWARD

That was over thirty years ago. The young man with no future, no direction and no hope turned everything over to God and never looked back. In the years to follow, Michael was taken under the wing of Calvary Chapel's senior pastor, Chuck Smith. Pastor Chuck and the elders of the church prayed over Michael and anointed him with oil, and his mind became completely healed. Michael began to study the Scriptures, minister to others, and learn to communicate God's love. Mike went on his own to San Diego to teach ten people in a home Bible Study. What began there as a small study, God has grown into a ministry that today reaches around the world with over 100 congregations, para-church organizations and home cell groups.

But the highlight of Michael's new life in Christ was God's healing of his marriage, and on April 3, 1971,

Michael watched Sandy walk down the aisle toward him again. As she did, he thought, '*Everything I destroyed. . . God is giving back to me. By rights I should be dead. But in spite of all the pills I swallowed and all the crazy things I did with my life, I'm healed. This is what being born again really means! I am nothing but a complete salvage operation, a sinner saved by grace.*'

Today Michael's preaching is at its zenith. He is the father of five, and a grandfather as well. God has led him to work with Billy Graham, teach in dozens of foreign countries, and expand his church tenfold. His church has evolved into Horizon International Ministries, and his festivals have changed thousands of lives for Christ the world over.

Just as He did for Michael, God has a tremendous life and ministry awaiting you if you will accept His forgiveness and follow Christ. Your life-change may not be as radical as Michael's, but it will be a complete transformation nonetheless.

To receive Jesus Christ as your Savior, you must
1. Admit your need for God (you are a sinner),
2. Be willing to turn from your sins to God,
3. Believe that Jesus Christ died for you on the cross and rose from the grave,
4. Pray to receive Jesus into your life.

HERE IS A SUGGESTED PRAYER:

Dear Jesus, I need you. I am a sinner and I need your forgiveness. I believe that you died to pay the penalty for my sins. I want to turn from my sins and follow you instead. I invite you to come into my heart and life. Amen.

Agape Papa

She finished reading this chapter and realized her grandfather had
written his spiritual journal to people who had not yet been born
(grandkids) by faith. Her eyes were watering from the dank dusty
attic. Her smeared mascara danced in pools of tears with the
decades old dust of her grandfather's attic. The sweaty back of her
wrists were charred with thin rings of soot. She hardly noticed and
could hardly turn the page fast enough to see what was next. She
soon discovered that God has great things planned for each and
every person's life.

FAITH FACTOR ONE

All of us must determine our philosophy of life or journey to faith.
Next, whom one chooses to follow leads to a commitment of faith.
Finally, in purposing to live a life by faith, we unlock the wonder
of living the Faith Factored life. Faith Factor One is this: Jesus
Christ is the key to everything. Ask Him to be your Savior by faith
today. If you know Jesus, ask someone else if they care to join you
in heaven.

FAITH FACTOR ONE IN ACTION

List three friends you will commit to pray for, sharing your life in
Jesus.

1.
2.
3.

FAITH FACTOR TWO

God Has Great Things Planned For You: Three Definitions of Faith

Beloved,

God has great things planned for you. Believe this!

> *"For I know the thoughts that I think toward you, says the Lord, thoughts of peace and not of evil, to give you a future and a hope."* **Jeremiah 29:11**

CHOICES

"Daddy, can I come with you?" Cade asked. "Yes!" I exclaimed. As I attempted unsuccessfully to hide my glee over Cade asking to join me at the local YMCA pool.

As we drove to the YMCA, I pondered how simple life is for Cade. At age six, all he has to say to me, his father, is simply, "Daddy, can I come with you?" The instant those words come out of his mouth and enter my ears, my whole world stops for him. God, our heavenly father, responds in an even more personal manner when we call upon his name in prayer by faith. *"Call to me, and I will answer you, and show you great and mighty things, which you do not know."* **Jeremiah 33:3**

God has great things planned for you and me. Like any good relationship, there is a period of introduction, becoming familiar with one another, choosing friendship, and the cultivating that friendship over the long haul. God has made us in His image. The purpose for our lives is to fellowship with God. We want this since He has great things planned for us.

Cade had been taking swimming lessons at the YMCA, mostly against his will. As parents, my wife and I knew this was an important skill for him to learn. Though he couldn't see the big picture, Cade had to trust we had his best interests in mind. Cade had to believe God's Word in **Jeremiah 29:11**, *"For I know the thoughts that I think toward you, says the Lord, thoughts of peace and not of evil, to give you a future and a hope."*

Slowly, over time, Cade was introduced to the water. First, by stepping in the shallow end. Later, he became familiar with the pool by holding on to the side. Next, he chose to become friendly with swimming by blowing bubbles. Later, quite surprisingly, Cade was choosing to cultivate his swimming skill by asking me, "Daddy, can I come with you?"

Our relationship with God often proceeds like Cade's swim lessons. The Lord introduces us to situations. Over time, he grows and encourages us. Soon we are given the privilege of encouraging others to grow and live for Christ. Real growth in Christ costs us something. Over time, Cade had experienced the good (floating), the bad (water up his nose), and the ugly (being dunked under water against his will). Our spiritual lives can resemble this type of growth. The question we should ask God is, "Am I still in your will, God?"

A willing heart is a prerequisite to grow in our relationship with God. We want to grow closer to God because we love Him and He has great things planned for us. On this day, my son Cade at age six had a willing heart. It was the first time he asked me to go swimming.

Cade and I had a wonderful time swimming. That day and each day thereafter for the next week, we went back to the YMCA to swim. Upon each visit, Cade and I grew closer together. Time spent with God will do that for us as well. Cade was also becoming more confident in the water.

I had been thinking that it was time for Cade to continue his growth by taking a big step of faith at our next YMCA visit. I asked Cade to stand up on the pool deck by the side and jump out to me. He was excited, at first. Then fear set in. Fear fought against faith. When fear overcomes faith, it can immobilize us. Cade stood frozen, fearful and teary- eyed. Cade needed a faith boost.

FAITH AND THE HEART OF GOD

The Bible tells us in **Romans 1:17**, *"The just shall live by faith."* In Hebrews 11:1 faith is defined as *"the substance of things hoped for, the evidence of things not seen."* In **Hebrews 11:6**, we are told, *"But without faith it is impossible to please him, for he who comes to God must believe that he is, and that he is a rewarder of those who diligently seek him."*

So, in essence, faith pleases God. A lack of faith is actually sin (see **Romans 14:23** and **Hebrews 10:37**). The best manner to grow in faith is reflected in **Romans 10:17**—*"so then faith comes by hearing, and hearing by the word of God."* When our faith wavers, we too can increase our faith by reading God's word, recording the stories of faith in other people's lives as well as remembering what God has done for us.

Frozen and sobbing, Cade was being strangled by fear. All I asked him to do was jump into my arms. In Cade's mind, I might as well have been asking him to jump off the moon.

Cade was facing a flashpoint of faith. He knew me, and he knew that I loved him. He knew enough about the water to convince him that if I didn't catch him something bad would ensue. He knew he was being asked to grow in his new swimming experience. God will do things often throughout each of our lives too. God requires all or nothing from us as we walk by faith.

Cade compromised. It is easier to compromise obedience to God than it is to walk by faith. Always. So like most of us, Cade sought the middle road. When we choose the middle road, more often than not, we get run over. Cade asked me to move closer. Then he asked me to reach up my hands so he could hold me as he jumped. Next, he got on his knees, then bottom, and finally wanted me to hold him as he slid from the pool deck into my arms. Fear had won over faith. And then the following thoughts occurred to me. Why did I want Cade to jump to me? What was the goal? How would it make Cade a better swimmer?

First, I wanted Cade to enjoy the fullness of swimming. Jumping from the side to his dad is fun. That is, once you get over the fear of jumping. God wants us to enjoy the fullness of life with Him too.

Second, I wanted Cade to jump so he could improve his swimming skills. He would also broaden his swimming experience. I hoped experience in the water would dispel his fears. I also wanted him to grow as a swimmer so that later in life he would live and not die because he hadn't learned to swim. God, too, wants us to live in Him and not die apart from Him.

Third, I had so many really neat things in store for Cade's future. Cade had to grow a step at a time improving his swimming skills. He also needed to grow through his fears. God has great things planned for you, too.

Here are some of what I had in mind as blessings for Cade:
-To jump off a diving board
-To swing out on a rope swing over a lake
-To go to a water park and slide all day in a wonderful water world
-To use a mask and snorkel while looking at beautifully colored fish and coral
-To learn to water ski
-To scuba dive
-To swim freely for pleasure
-To ride jet skis
-To surf or boogie board
-Much more!

Consider for a moment the blessings you and I may be missing simply by not obeying God's (our Father's) voice. How much frustration in our lives can be eliminated in trusting by faith the command or plan of God (our Father)? What can we do? How do we get started walking by faith and trusting God?

To begin, read God's word. Study the stories of people in the Bible who have walked by faith. Increase your faith by memorizing the faith life of others. Next, pray and ask God to give you a vision and call for your life. Finally, obey what God puts in front of you one step at a time.

It took two more weeks, but Cade finally jumped to me. He stood on the side, I was in the middle of the pool, and he jumped out to me. It took all he had to reach me. His toes pushed off the side, his legs thrust forward and his arms outstretched were about two feet short of where I was standing. Cade had a flashpoint of faith.

I stood firm. Cade landed, splashed, kicked, paddled, gasped and grabbed me. He clung to me actually. He smiled, laughed, thanked me, and pushed off from me to go back and do it again. I spent the next few hours responding to a one-word joyous request from my six-year-old son. "Again, again, again."

God has great things planned for you. Today is a perfect day to pray, trust, and obey God's voice in your life. Remember, God is in love with you. He has left you and me a journal (The Bible) that we can read that tells us of His love and care for us. Let's believe Him today.

"For I know the thoughts that I think toward you, says the Lord, thoughts of peace and not of evil, to give you a future and a hope."
Jeremiah 29:11

KNOWING GOD'S WILL

Wait a minute, you may ask. What if what I desire is not what God desires to give me? What do I do then? Let's check the directions (Bible) for a clue. In **Matthew 6:33** we are told, *"Seek first the kingdom of God and His righteousness and all these things will be added to you."*

In answering the question of our desires being God's desire, we must consider our motives. If we want things more than we want God, this is not helpful for us. Next, we need to notice whether or not we get upset each time we don't get our own way. It may be that *"you ask and do not receive, because you ask amiss, that you may spend it on your pleasures"* **James 4:3** is true of us. Likewise, perhaps God wants us to wait for now. Waiting often produces patience. In **James 1:2-4**, we are told, *"My brethren, count it all joy when you fall into various trials, knowing that the testing of your faith produces patience. But let patience have its perfect work, that you may be perfect and complete, lacking nothing."*

Patience usually means putting up with our shortcomings in some-one we love. Getting old produces patience. Older couples have an entirely unique view of faith-producing patience. In the following story, from my friend Bob Johnson, we see faith and patience producing a humorous outcome.

> 70-year-old George went for his annual physical. All of his tests came back with normal results. Dr. Smith said, 'George, everything looks great physically. How are you doing mentally and emotionally? Are you at peace with yourself, and do you have a good relationship with God?'
>
> George replied, 'God and me are tight. He knows I have poor eyesight, so He's fixed it so that when I get up in the middle of the night to go to the bathroom (poof!), the light goes on when I pee, and (poof!), the light goes off when I'm done.'
>
> 'Wow!' Exclaimed Dr. Smith, 'that's incredible!'
>
> A little later in the day Dr. Smith called George's wife. 'Thelma,' he said, 'George is just fine. Physically he is great. But I had to call because I'm in awe of his relationship with God. Is it true that he gets up during the night and (poof!) the light goes on in the bathroom, and then (poof!), the light goes off when he finishes?'
>
> Thelma was silent, somewhat startled and exclaimed, 'That old fool! He's peeing in the refrigerator again!'
>
> *Author Unknown*

If you have a hard time figuring out God's will in answering your prayers, consider for a moment the demoniac in Mark chapter five. Here was a man possessed by many demons: he had cut himself, people would not go near him, his loneliness must have been crushing. Jesus comes near, and the man cries out. Jesus heals him of the demons and sends the demons into a herd of swine. When Jesus gets into a boat to leave the place, the very first, the FIRST prayer out of the man's mouth to Jesus is to beg to come with Him, and Jesus says NO! *"And when He got into the boat, he who had been demon-possessed begged Him that he might be with him. However Jesus did not permit him, but said to him, 'Go home to your friends, and tell them what great things the Lord has done for you, and how He has had compassion on you'"* **Mark 5:18-20**.

If you are having a hard time trying to figure out the Lord's will, consider the poor demon-possessed man. This is one of those moments when everything rational can end up right out the window if we are not careful. To begin with, Jesus did answer the demons' request to be cast into the swine. However, the man possessed did not get a "yes" to his first prayer. I wonder how he felt when he was told he had to stay behind, not get into the boat with Jesus, and head back home to people who had most certainly given up on him or even ridiculed him and mocked him. I suppose a simple bewilderment must have covered his face as he considered Jesus saying "yes" to his demons but "no" to his simple and seemingly admirable wish to stay in Jesus' presence.

The bottom line is that the previously possessed man would be a "living epistle" to all who knew him upon his return to his home. Since he was now radically changed, that alone would give him the authority and platform to proclaim the truth of Jesus Christ. In his case it would have been wasted time to sit with Jesus any longer. In fact many others would eventually listen to the truth of Christ only because of the irrefutable proof of Jesus' power in the life of this man. They could see the change in him.

In the end we may rest in the Word of God. *"'For My thoughts are not your thoughts, Nor are your ways My ways,' says the Lord. 'For as the heavens are higher than the earth, So are My ways higher than your ways, and My thoughts than your thoughts.'"* **Isaiah 55:8-9**

In considering faith, we can be certain of how to proceed. God has left us his roadmap, the Bible. The Bible gives us clear guidance in the area of faith.

THREE DEFINITIONS OF FAITH

The three guidelines or definitions of faith are simple:

1. *Hebrews 11:1*—Faith is your hope in spite of circumstances. It is trusting that God will bring the best out of whatever situation you find yourself in, no matter what. *"Faith is the assurance of things hoped for, the conviction of things not seen."*

2. *Hebrews 11:6*—Faith is the only way to please God. *"But without faith it is impossible to please Him, for he who comes to God must believe that He is, and that He is a rewarder of those who diligently seek Him."*

3. *Romans 14:23*— Faithlessness is sin, which separates us from God. *"...whatever is not of faith is sin."*

Interestingly, faith requires action. The Bible says *"Thus also faith by itself, if it does not have works is dead."* *James 2:17* Thus, as we read God's word, we begin to live a greater faith. Consider Martin Luther King Jr.'s testimony of faith.

By January 1956, with the Montgomery bus boycott in full swing, threatening phone calls, up to 40 a day, began pouring into King's home. Though he put up a strong front, the threats unsettled him. One midnight as he sat over a cup of coffee worrying, the phone rang again, and the caller said, 'Nigger, we are tired of you and your mess now. And if you aren't out of this town in three days, we're going to blow your brains out and blow up your house.' King later described what happened in the next few minutes:

'I sat there and thought about a beautiful little daughter who had just been born.... She was the darling of my life. I'd come in night after night and see that gentle little smile. And I sat at that table thinking about that little girl and thinking about the fact that she could be taken away from me any minute.

'And I started thinking about a dedicated, devoted, and loyal wife, who was over there asleep. And she could be taken from me, or I could be taken from her. And I got to the point where I couldn't take it any longer. I was weak...

'And I discovered then that religion had to become real to me, and I had to know God for myself. And I bowed down over that cup of coffee. I will never forget it.... I prayed a prayer, and I prayed out loud that night. I said, 'Lord, I'm down here trying to do what's right. I think I'm right. I think the cause we represent is right. But Lord, I must confess that I'm weak now. I'm faltering. I'm losing my courage. And I can't let the people see me like this because if they see me weak and losing my courage, they will begin to get weak....'

'And it seemed at that moment that I could hear an inner voice saying to me, "Martin Luther, stand up for righteousness. Stand up for justice. Stand up for truth. And lo I will be with you, even until the end of the world".... Almost at once my fears began to go. My uncertainty disappeared.'

The three guidelines or definitions of faith beg the question, "How do we improve or increase our faith?" The best way to increase our faith is to read God's Word, the Bible. *"So faith comes by hearing, and hearing by the word of God."* **Romans 10:17**

ABIDE

Another interesting facet of faith is that it abides in God. *"And now abide faith, hope, love, these three...."* **1 Corinthians 13:13** Now as long as we are abiding in Christ, good things will eventuate. The "8:28" is still in effect. *"And we know all things work together for* *good to those who love God, to those who are called according to His purpose. " **Romans 8:28** We can stop worrying now. In fact, if we would pray each time we sensed a need to worry, we would see amazing things happen in our lives and the lives of those we pray for. Things work out beautifully if we will simply abide.

An abiding faith is a relaxed faith. Abiding faith simply obeys the moment-by-moment faith choices as they are presented. Abiding faith says "yes" to the homeless man. It says, "I will not only give you something for the road like the hat on my head, but I will take you to a restaurant and buy you lunch while I share Jesus with you." Abiding faith reflects God's glory by calling a sister or cousin and apologizing first thing in the morning for something wrong I had done or said. Abiding faith thanks God for the privilege of serving people who are not appreciating all we do and in some instances stab us in the back with gossip, slander, and hateful innuendo.

Here is a true story that speaks to abiding in hope by faith, **Hebrews 11:1** activating faith, **Hebrews 11:6** then waiting by faith while someone else's sin or faithlessness **Romans 10:17** caused a time of waiting, and waiting, and waiting....

> I was an idiot! I met this beautiful girl on a mission trip to Grenada in the Caribbean. We had a natural attraction toward one another. We prayed, read the Bible together, and desired to draw closer to God. I just couldn't make a commitment.
>
> I understand now that fear of commitment is quite common with men in relationships. At the time however I thought in my paralysis I was just a fool. I should have asked this girl to marry me after about a year or so of courting. However, instead I just dropped out of the relationship "cold" in hopes of "finding God's will" elsewhere. Dumb!

So for four years or so I served in ministry, went on other mission trips, prayed hard for God to reveal the wife for me, and the whole time she was right in front of me. In my fear and unbelief, I just couldn't believe it would be so easy and such a blessing. Like most guys I wondered if there was anyone else out there. I was also afraid of the responsibility. So I made her wait four more years in a type of wilderness experience for me to grow in my faith. I was an idiot.

During this time the girl was faithful. She went on to study more of God at a School of Evangelism, she served in the ministry, she prayed and waited, and waited, and waited.... My lack of obedience to God caused her to have to wait. So selfish on my part.

My struggles revolved around having no peace when dealing with anyone of the opposite sex during this time of rebellion. Also, I had a sense that life was slipping away from me. Likewise, thoughts of inadequacy swam through my mind on a continual basis. In short, I was miserable.

The beautiful girl tried to move on. God gave her a choice though. She chose to wait for me to get a clue; this was her faith walk. In waiting, she had to deal with rejection, and for a woman it is a cruel and bitter walk down a chilly and icy landscape.

Years later, as I counseled a young man regarding the very subject of love and commitment, I realized that fear of commitment is a very common malady among Christians. I told this young man that from my experience his lack of commitment and sin of faithlessness was not only hurting him but causing much grief for some young lady. I shared with him that when we do not walk by faith, in this case in the area of love, our sin (lack of faith) can cause hurt in other people's lives. I noted that as he was praying for God's wife for him, he needed to do his part faithfully to be prepared for God's answer.

Somewhere out in the world today was a young lady praying, fasting, and reading her Bible, waiting on God to reveal whom He had chosen for her to marry. In this case that man was my friend I was counseling. The only problem was my friend was nowhere near ready. In fact if God had introduced them at this point, my friend's hang-ups would probably have killed the deal. So my friend lingers in fear and the young lady waits, and waits, and waits....

I have discovered from my own life, and the lives of others, that each of us needs to obey God by faith, when He presents choices to us. We may feel inadequate, ill-prepared, or simply terrified. It doesn't matter; obey. The lives of others are directly affected by what we choose to do, either by faith, or by fear.

My friend has begun to deal with his fears. He realizes now that God is excited about "hooking him up." He also realizes that whoever God has for him may already be ready. It just might be that my friend is the reason the blessing from God is in the waiting room. Interestingly, as he prepares by faith to be all God wants him to be, he will become more Christ-like and therefore more desirable to the young lady when the time comes to actually meet and have the "eyes of their hearts opened" to one another.

One day I decided that the hurt and narrowness of my life in sin needed to stop. So I prayed and asked God to go on a walk of faith with me. I prayed that God would help me make this commitment to the beautiful young girl I had met over five years previously. I wasn't very mature, so I asked God to give me a series of signs along the walk.

In every instance, God met and exceeded my prayers for discovering that this girl had indeed been set aside for me by God. I had not really seen the beautiful girl for most of the last four years. The exceptions were that anytime I was with another girl, God had the beautiful girl and I end up at the same place at the oddest times and locations. It was weird. God had to have been laughing out loud.

I was so focused on God and His will for the beautiful girl and me that once I got to the end of my prayer list and all my fleeces were answered, I was finally ready for action. So I called the beautiful girl up, asked her to dinner; she accepted. We took a walk on the beach at sunset. We stopped and then the waiting was over. I simply smiled at her and handed her my Baltimore Orioles hat which she looked at in bemusement. I was so nervous all I could do was point and hope she turned the bill of the cap right-side up. She did and read the following words in stunned silence, "Will you marry me?" I now waited. The beautiful girl smiled and cried. I got on my knee and held her hand as I actually mouthed the words and then we hugged. Standing in front of the Hotel Del Coronado, caught up in a majestic November sunset, we held each other and prayed. The beach was completely empty as the chilly fall winds whipped across the glimmering pacific. The sun was setting in a glorious resplendence that took our breath away. Just then a jogger appeared literally out of nowhere.

We looked at one another, then at the man who said the following to us: "The glory of the Lord will shine on your marriage." "Wow!" we thought as we looked into each other's eyes for a brief moment. Then turning back to thank the man we discovered he had vanished! Gone and no trace of another person on the beach at all. God had met us in our moment of faith.

Interestingly, and I am sure not surprising to women reading this, it was seven years into my marriage to the beautiful girl that it dawned on me that she had to have HUGE faith that day on the beach to say yes to my proposal. I was so focused on God and His will for our lives that once He had answered all my prayers, it never dawned on me the beautiful girl would say no. I never considered it odd that a man would ask a girl to marry him after not dating for four years and not really speaking for over a year. I just knew God had great things planned for me. Finally, I had decided to receive them by faith. That's the power of faith available to you today.

Agape Papa

In reading her grandfather's journal entry the young woman really sensed God has great things planned for everyone. She sensed her grandfather would want to say trust God. Trust Him! Her knees began to ache from sitting in such close quarters for so long. A thin sweaty drop oozed from her left leg just behind the kneecap. Time stood still for now. She could hardly wait to discover the three stages of faith to help better know God's will in chapter three of her grandfather's spiritual journal.

FAITH FACTOR TWO

Faith Factor Two encourages us with the truth that God has great things planned for us. Faith Factor Two defines Biblical faith. Faith is our hope in spite of circumstances, trusting that God will bring it about. Faith is the only thing that can please God. Whatever is not of faith is sin. Increase your faith by reading the Bible.

Believe God for big things in your life. Remember God has great things planned for you!

FAITH FACTOR TWO IN ACTION

List three things God has promised you. Write them down even if you can't believe (by faith) that He will bring them to pass.

1.
2.
3.

Faith and Knowing
God's Will: Three Stages of Faith

Beloved,

Know God's will by knowing God. *"Now it came to pass after these things that God tested Abraham, and said to him, 'Abraham!' And he said, 'Here I am.'"* **Genesis 22:1**

The gospel is not a truth among other truths. Rather, it sets a question mark against all truths.

Karl Barth

Dietrich Bonhoeffer gave his life in pursuit of the gospel. He alone during the height of Nazi domination in his homeland of Germany opposed the intrusion of Hitler's politics within the country's churches. He would not compromise. He spent time in jail and died early, too early, as a martyr for Jesus Christ. Few people know that his first inclination was to flee the injustice rather than stand and fight for what he believed was right. The following is a letter that helped him impact the cause of Christ in perilous times.

In 1933, Karl Barth wrote his discouraged colleague Dietrich Bonhoeffer who, disgusted with the German Christian response to Hitler, fled Germany to pastor a German-speaking parish in England.

"What is all this about 'going away,' and 'quietness of pastoral work,' etc., at a moment when you are wanted in Germany? You, who know as well as I do that the opposition in Berlin and the opposition of the church in Germany as a whole stands inwardly on such weak feet! Why aren't you always there where so much could depend on there being a couple of game people on the watch on every occasion, great or small, and trying to save what there is to be saved?

"I think I can see from your letter that you, like all of us—yes, all of us!—are suffering under the quite common difficulty of taking 'certain steps' in the present chaos, that we are rather required in and with our uncertainty, even if we should stumble or go wrong ten times or a hundred times, to do our bit?

"One simply cannot become weary now. Still less can one go to England! What in all the world would you want to do there?… You must now leave go of all these intellectual flourishes and special considerations, however interesting they may be, and think of only one thing, that you are a German, that the house of your church is on fire, that you know enough to be able to help, and that you must return to your post by the next ship."

Bonhoeffer returned to Germany 16 months later, after Karl Barth had been exiled to Switzerland.

It is interesting to note that like Bonhoeffer, I often seem to want to flee the faith opportunities that present themselves to me on a daily basis. I pray that as I grow closer to our Lord I will choose His plan for my life. He has so much more in store for me and it is probably not the road most traveled. I am sure, beloved, that it has everything to do with faith. I have always wondered about the process of faith.

I sought out wisdom by reading Scripture. Along the way, I heard a sermon by Charles Stanley on the three stages of faith. Here is what I learned about faith and knowing God's will.

LITTLE FAITH

First, there is little faith. This is a restless faith. Little faith asks, "God can do it, but will He?" Can you imagine Abraham when God started to speak to him of a son and being the father of many nations?

In **Genesis 17:1-9**, the Bible lays out a promise of eternal proportions. As you read this, know God has something just as grand and wonderful for you too.

> *"When Abram was ninety-nine years old, the Lord appeared to Abram and said to him, 'I am Almighty God; walk before me and be blameless. And I will make my covenant between me and you, and will multiply you exceedingly.' Then Abram fell on his face, and God talked with him, saying, 'As for me, behold, my covenant is with you, and you shall be a father of many nations. No longer shall your name be called Abram, but your name shall be Abraham; for I have made you a father of many nations. I will make you exceedingly fruitful; and I will make nations of you, and kings shall come from you. And I will establish my covenant between me and you and your descendants after you in their generations, for an everlasting covenant, to be God to you and your descendants after you. Also I give to you and your descendants after you the land in which you are a stranger, all the land of Canaan, as an everlasting possession; and I will be their God.' And God said to Abraham: 'As for you, you shall keep my covenant, you and your descendants after you throughout their generations.'"*

Has God given you promises like these? Do you think you are too old or too young to receive God's promise for you? Has God promised to multiply your education, money, or relationships? Is it amazing to you? Has God told you that many, many people will be affected by your being blessed by God? Do you trust God to make you fruitful, to give you the land that seems impossible right now?

If you are having a hard time receiving the blessings of God, you are not alone. Consider Abraham's "little faith" response to God's treasure chest of promises.

> *"Then Abraham fell on his face and laughed, and said in his heart, 'Shall a child be born to a man who is one hundred years old? And shall Sarah, who is ninety years old bear a child?'"* **Genesis 17:17**

Abraham's little faith focused on the logical, rational, and experiential information at his sensory level of understanding. He was walking by knowledge and doubt, not by faith. However, Abraham was teachable. He was willing to grow into the promises of God for himself and his family. How about you and me? Are we teachable and open to growing into God's promises for our lives?

GREAT FAITH

Next, Abraham grew from little faith to great faith. He saw his faith as reaching out and believing that God can do it and indeed that God will do it. Abraham began to have a relationship with God. God was his father and friend. As such, Abraham began to live supernaturally as if it were obviously the thing to do. Consider the following encounter from *Genesis 18:1-3*.

> *"Then the Lord appeared to him [Abraham] by the terebinth trees of Mamre, as he was sitting in the tent door in the heat of the day. So he lifted his eyes and looked, and behold, three men were standing by him; and when he saw them, he ran from the tent door to meet them, and bowed himself to the ground."*

Wow! What happened to good old Abe? He had grown from laughing and doubting God to running toward God at a supernatural appearance in the heat of the day. Isn't that exciting? You and I can grow in trust and faith with God—just as Abraham did.

Shortly after the experience with God in the desert, Abraham graduates from the school of great faith to perfect faith. In *Genesis 18:16-33*, Abraham begins to intercede on behalf of Sodom and Gomorrah. He actually begins negotiating with God by faith. *Genesis 18:23* says, *"And Abraham came near and said, 'Would you also destroy the righteous with the wicked?'"*

Later, in *Genesis 18:32-33*, *"Then he said, 'Let not the Lord be angry, and I will speak but once more: Suppose ten should be found there?' And he said, 'I will not destroy it for the sake of ten.' So the Lord went his way as soon as he had finished speaking with Abraham; and Abraham returned to his place."*

PERFECT FAITH

Perfect faith is a resting faith. It moves past little faith, a restless faith that says, "God can do it, but will He?" It moves beyond great faith, a reaching-out faith that states God can do it and He **will** do it. Perfect faith rests and simply believes that it is already done.

In *Genesis 22:1-18*, we see the fulfillment of Abraham's growth in perfect faith and knowing God's will for his life.

"Now it came to pass after these things that God tested Abraham, and said to him, 'Abraham!' And he said, 'Here I am.' Then he said, 'Take now your son, your only son Isaac, whom you love and go to the land of Moriah, and offer him there as a burnt offering on one of the mountains of which I shall tell you.' So Abraham rose early in the morning and saddled his donkey, and took two of his young men

with him, and Isaac his son; and he split the wood for the burnt offering, and arose and went to the place of which God had told him. Then on the third day Abraham lifted his eyes and saw the place afar off. And Abraham said to his young men, 'Stay here with the donkey; the lad and I will go yonder and worship, and we will come back to you.' So Abraham took the wood of the burnt offering and laid it on Isaac his son; and he took the fire in his hands, and a knife, and the two of them when together. But Isaac spoke to Abraham his father and said, 'My father!' And he said, 'Here I am, my son.' Then he said, 'Look the fire and the wood, but where is the lamb for a burnt offering?' And Abraham said, 'My son, God will provide for himself the lamb for a burnt offering.' So the two of them went together. Then they came to the place of which God had told him. And Abraham built an altar there and placed the wood in order and he bound Isaac his son and laid him on the altar, upon the wood. And Abraham stretched out his hand and took the knife to slay his son. But the Angel of the Lord called to him from heaven and said, 'Abraham, Abraham!' So he said, 'Here I am.' And he said, 'Do not lay your hand on the lad or do anything to him; for now I know that you fear God since you have not withheld your son, your only son, from me.' Then Abraham lifted his eyes and looked, and there behind him was a ram caught in a thicket by its horns. So Abraham went and took the ram, and offered it up for a burnt offering instead of his son. And Abraham called the name of the place, The-Lord-Will-Provide; as it is said to this day, 'In the Mount of the Lord it shall be provided.' Then the Angel of the Lord called to Abraham a second time out of heaven, and said, 'By myself I have sworn, says the Lord, because you have done this thing, and have not withheld your son, your only son, in blessing I will bless you, and multiplying I will multiply your descendants as the stars of heaven and as the sand which is on the seashore; and your descendants shall possess the gate of their enemies. In your seed all the nations of the earth shall be blessed, because you have obeyed my voice.'"

My prayer for you and myself is that, like Abraham running from his tent to greet a supernatural God visiting in the heat of the day, you and I would believe and receive all God has for us and our families. God can do it. He wants to do it. He will do it. The Lord of the universe wants to meet, talk, walk with, and bless you. Today. Believe it.

The three stages of faith according to Charles Stanley are these:
1. Little faith—this is a restless faith. Little faith asks, "God can do it but will He?
2. Great faith—this is a reaching-out faith. Great faith asserts, "God can do it and He will do it."
3. Perfect faith—this is a resting faith. Perfect faith rests and simply believes it is already done.

STAGES OF FAITH

Tom is a local Pastor of a small church of about 30 full time attendees. He is growing in his faith. His church needed a projector to show the words of the songs for worship on the screen so folks could learn the words. By faith Tom prayed to God for help.

Ordinarily, Tom would have also done the following:
1. Little faith—put an appeal in the bulletin
2. Great faith—suggest from the pulpit the importance of the need
3. Perfect faith—pray and wait on God

This time Tom purposed in his heart to simply ask God for the need. All week he prayed, asked no one, didn't even give a hint (not even, "hey brother, I have a prayer request..."). What happened next was, well, faith in action.

Since the church met in a room rented from the local service club, it wasn't until Sunday that God's provision became apparent to all. First, the worship leader was given a brand new projection screen from a larger church early in the week. He didn't know what to do with it but a still voice in his head told him to just take it to church on Sunday, which he did.

Second, on Wednesday someone else dropped off two used screens and a projector at the service club addressed to the church with no return address. Finally, in the sermon that Sunday Tom revealed God's provision by faith to the congregation. What he didn't know was that God had more in store for Tom's faith.

The new screen the church would use. The two used screens and projector would be split between a mid-week study and children's ministry at the women's club. It seemed Tom had faith for one screen for the adults. God had in store better quality for the mid-week study, which was at a different location, as well as the children's ministry.

Something else happened too. While preaching, Tom shared about the three screens and projector. He shared how by faith he was committed to praying first from now on for all his personal and church needs. When he praised God for His provision, someone in the seats pointed behind the stage and yelled, "another blessing!"

Tom was astounded and a little awestruck. He had prayed for a single projector screen. He had asked God by faith. He had told no one else. God had not only answered his need for one screen, but had expanded the ministry by a factor of four and given the church an opportunity for ministry beyond themselves. The fifth screen would be given to a church in Mexico they would be ministering to the following weekend. By faith God's blessing to Tom would now overflow unto others who perhaps had no idea it was coming. Is your faith an overflowing faith?

Perhaps you cannot figure out what, if anything, God has promised you. How can you tell if your desires are God's desires? Everyone struggles with these questions at one time or another. Here is a simple checklist that may help.

FAITH CHECKLIST

First, remember to study God's Word. Study the Bible by asking questions such as these: "Is this story relevant to my life? Is this a scripture promise to me now? Do the characters of the people in the story reflect truth in my own life?" Also, while meditating or memorizing a scripture, ask yourself, "is God putting an idea or impression on my mind from this scripture?"

Next, consider God's character. God is just, loving, faithful, wise, truthful, and so much more. Since we can count on God's character, we know He loves us, has a plan for us, made us in His image, and will therefore give us great confidence "*. . .that He who has begun a good work in you will complete it until the day of Jesus Christ.*" **Philippians 1:6.**

Third, trust God's Son. Jesus said, "*I have come that they may have life, and that they may have it more abundantly.*" **John 10:10** This abundant life is not a "name it and claim it" type of thing. Instead it is a simple, sincere trust that Jesus' death was not in vain, and that my place in this world is meaningful, designed to reflect God's glory, and important to God. I trust that my purpose fills a specific niche that God has prepared for me before I was even born.

Try to focus on these three areas. Spend time in God's Word, trust God's character, believe in God's Son Jesus Christ. Perhaps you will now start to journal important ideas, insights and experiences daily. Find a friend or pastor to pray with you. Be patient with yourself. In due time, God's many promises will be revealed to you. The life God has given us is as fulfilling in the journey stage as it is in the destination stage. Relax, you are doing fine.

Agape Papa

The lovely young lady was riveted. Her back slouching over the journal for so long felt like it had two railroad ties nailed to it. When she moved, her back muscles revolted in searing pain. She was tired. Tired not just of sitting but of life, her life. Her time in the dirty, dark, time-worn attic seemed to be a metaphor for her life as it was. Just one more chapter the girl pondered. Then inside her heart the thought occurred. Check out the three keys to unlocking your faith next!

FAITH FACTOR THREE

Faith Factor Three encourages us in our faith and in knowing God's will. Faith Factor Three is about the stages of faith. Our faith grows from little faith to great faith to perfect faith. Rejoice in the process of growth. Different situations will present different stages of faith for us to grow through. Relax, it's a relationship, not a race.

FAITH FACTOR THREE IN ACTION

Identify one area of your life that fits each stage of faith.

    1. Little faith—

    2. Great faith—

    3. Perfect faith—

Now pray God moves in a personal way in each of these areas of your life. Trust Him!

A.S.K.:
Three Keys to Faith

Beloved,

Sometimes you have to ask to get the blessing. *"Ask and you will receive whatever you ask for that your joy may be made full."* **John 14:14b**

A LESSON IN FAITH

Today my mother, my sons Cade and Cana, ages six and three, and I went to lunch at a local sandwich shop. It was a little after 11 a.m. The sky was a dull gray in late December. It was a lazy Saturday morning. I was not in a particularly spiritual mindset. We were just looking for a little lunch.

In ordering for the boys, I chose the children's meal pack. As with most restaurants, the kid's meal included a toy. Since I was an experienced father by now, I wisely purchased one kid's meal for each boy. I also made sure each meal had the same toy. I hoped this would prevent the trauma of comparisons between the boys as to who got the better toy.

We prayed for our meal. We ate with minimal fanfare. We shared a bag of chips. We shared two cookies between four of us. This was wonderful. Then we opened the toys.

Luke 11:9 says, *"So I say to you ask and it will be given to you...."* I began to see immediately the wisdom of this scripture. First, we must ask God for what we believe He would want for us. Children understand the power of asking.

Unexplainably, the toys had no directions. Since Cade wanted to know how the toys worked (a six-year-old's perspective), he began to ask over and over, "Daddy, how does this work?" Cana, at age three, took great care to underscore, word for word, exactly what Cade had just asked. A lazy, quiet, and peaceful Saturday lunch was suddenly becoming stressful.

I noticed rather quickly that the more Cade asked, "Daddy, how does this work?," the more tense I became. As Cana parroted Cade's inquiries, my patience wavered further. I was amazed at how quickly I allowed my peace of mind to be diminished just by circumstances changing ever so slightly.

I needed a quick exit strategy. I thought for another few minutes and decided it would be best if we all just left. I knew we had no directions for their toys. We had tried every possible combination to make them work. It was time to surrender, honorably, but move on nonetheless.

Cade, however, had more perseverance. The second area of focus in our faith walk is that we must seek God repetitively. In seeking God over and over the intent is not to get something from God; it is to bring God into something we feel is important. We need to seek the face of God, not the hand of God. Children understand that wherever their father is, the blessing is sure to follow.

So I suggested we leave and go home and ride our bikes. I had the trash in the garbage before I heard the words, "Daddy, let's ask somebody." What? I thought. "Daddy, let's ask somebody to show us how these toys work," Cade persisted. "Daddy, ask somebody," Cana joined in with him.

I froze. Pride took over and I thought, "We don't need to ask any-one how to make these toys work." Then I realized we had spent half an hour trying to figure out how the toys worked to no avail. "Daddy, let's ask somebody." Cade persisted. The door was within grasp at this point. "Daddy, ask somebody," Cana reminded me. I froze.

The third area of focus needs to be a continual knocking. Often when we knock on someone's door, our knock will grow increasingly louder the longer we knock. God understands this. The longer and harder we knock, the more focused we become on the object of our knocking and what we are knocking for. Children understand that sometimes the knocking in and of itself can become the blessing.

Finally, I realized that my pride was getting in the way of Cade and Cana's potentially being blessed with a toy that actually worked. So I said, "Let's go ask." So we did. The manager was gracious and polite but quickly disappeared into the back and out of sight. I had a sense the manager might not have known much more about the operation of the toy than we did.

I was wrong. I was humbled. I was amazed. The manager came out with a handful of toys. She set the toys on the counter and we watched as she began to connect each piece. Cade's eyes were as big as saucers. Cana's mouth was wide open.

The manager explained how each piece fit together and had a special part to play to make the toy work properly. It turned out we had actually been given only one part of a four piece toy set. The marketing strategy required customers (that included us) to come back at least four times to complete the toy in such a way that it would actually work.

The manager finished setting the last piece in place. She clicked a button and a light went on. She spun a disk and a sound came out. Cade's eyes lit up. Cana squealed, "Look, look, our toy works!" I smiled. Truly, the best was right at hand.

Like so much else in our lives with God, the best was saved for last. As I watched Cade and Cana marvel at their toy (blessing) coming together before their eyes, I thought how close I had come to missing this. My pride, impatience, and selfishness nearly got in the way of something with which God wanted to bless my boys.

The manager finished putting the toy together. She handed it to Cade and said, "You may have this." Cade marveled and said, "Daddy, look! We got four toys and now our toy works like it's supposed to." I smiled. Cade said, "Thank you." My mom and I also said, "Thank you." The manager replied, "It is my pleasure."

Driving home I listened to the cackles, giggles and joy emanating from my boys and their new toy in the back seat. I was amazed. I knew once again that God was speaking to me through my sons. I pondered what I had just experienced. I wanted to give God a chance to teach me all he had for me in this situation.

First, I realized I could and probably did miss God's blessings because of my pride, impatience, selfishness and unbelief. Second, when I humbled myself by faith, God's blessings would be unleashed in unpredictable ways. Third, like my son Cade, if I will simply be willing to "Ask" God for things with persistence and a pure heart, He will often respond by doing *". . .exceedingly abundantly above all that we ask or think." **Ephesians 3:20***

I considered how simply this all started. Cade simply wanted to know how his toy worked. He had the faith to ask someone to help him know how his toy worked. He was persistent. Learning how his toy worked in connection with three other pieces rewarded his faith and humility. He was ultimately blessed in an amazing, personal way as the manager gave him all four toy pieces working together. Cade and Cana were very blessed.

God wants to bless you and me this same way. I learned something special from my sons this day. In essence, we have to ask to get the blessing. God has given His personal promise on this matter. *"Ask and you will receive that your joy may be made full."* **John 14:14**

Today, you and I have a choice. God is possibly giving us one small piece of something that seems like a nice blessing. It may not be working correctly yet, like Cade's toy. He may be asking us to walk by faith in some manner related to our piece of the puzzle. When we choose faith in God and humbly walk with Him, unexplainable and unforeseen blessings await us. We just need to remember the simplicity of the lesson I learned from Cade. You have to ask to get the blessing.

KEYS TO FAITH

Here are the three keys to faith:

1. ASK for God's blessing in your life. In *1 Chronicles 4:9-10* Jabez did. *"Oh that you would bless me indeed, and enlarge my territory, that your hand would be with me, and that you would keep me from evil, that I might not cause pain! So God granted him what he requested."* Did you catch the last sentence?

2. SEEK the Lord with all your heart. ***Deuteronomy 6:4-5*** says, *"Hear O Israel: the Lord our God, the Lord is One. You shall love the Lord your God with all your heart, with all your soul, and with all your strength."*

3. KNOCK on the Lord's heart for the burden He has given you. ***Nehemiah 1: 4*** says, *"So it was, when I heard these words, that I sat down and wept, and mourned for many days; I was fasting and praying before the God of heaven."*

Remember the key: Ask, Seek, and Knock—these are really just a series of verbs.   Faith is a verb.   Faith requires action.   Faith requires action from you and me today.   At the end of Nehemiah's request of the king, he is asked the following, *"...then the King said to me what do you request?"*

If faith is a verb and requires us to keep asking, keep seeking, and keep knocking, doesn't it stand to reason that faith works the exact same way with God toward us?   Doesn't God say He "stands at the door knocking…" ?   Didn't God wait for you and me to say "yes" to His invitation for salvation?   Doesn't God ask us over and over just to do something simple to obey Him so we can be blessed to be in His presence and reap the fruit of an obedient life?

THE GIFT OF FAITH

What if God were asking you right now, "what do you request?" How would you respond?   Here is the fruit of a prayerful faith.   It is from someone who understands that at the end of the day faith is a gift from God.   This story was shared by my friend Bob Johnson.

The Weight of Prayer

     Louise Redden, a poorly dressed lady with a look of defeat on her face, walked into a grocery store.   She approached the owner of the store in a most humble manner and asked if he would let her charge a few groceries.

     She softly explained that her husband was very ill and unable to work, they had seven children and they needed food.   John Longhouse, the grocer, scoffed at her and requested that she leave his store. Visualizing the family needs, she said, *'Please, sir! I will bring you the money just as soon as I can.'*

     John told her he could not give her credit, as she did not have a charge account at his store.

Standing beside the counter was a customer who overheard the conversation between the two. The customer walked forward and told the grocerman that he would stand good for whatever she needed for her family. The grocerman said in a very reluctant voice, 'Do you have a grocery list?' Louise replied 'Yes sir!'

'O.K.' the grocer said: 'Put your grocery list on the scales and whatever your grocery list weighs, I will give you that amount in groceries.' Louise hesitated a moment with a bowed head, then she reached into her purse and took out a piece of paper and scribbled something on it. She then laid the piece of paper on the scale carefully with her head still bowed.

The eyes of the grocerman and the customer showed amazement when the scales went down and stayed down. The grocerman staring at the scales turned slowly to the customer and said begrudgingly, *'I can't believe it.'*

The customer smiled and the grocerman started putting the groceries on the other side of the scales. The scale did not balance so he continued to put more and more groceries on them until the scales would hold no more. The grocerman stood there in utter disgust. Finally, he grabbed the piece of paper from the scales and looked at it with greater amazement.

It was not a grocery list, it was a prayer, which said: *'Dear Lord, you know my needs and I am leaving this in your hands.'* The grocerman gave her the groceries that he had gathered and placed on the scales and stood in stunned silence.

Louise thanked him and left the store. The customer handed a fifty-dollar bill to John as he

said, *'It was worth every penny of it.'* It was sometime later that John Longhouse discovered the scales
were broken; therefore only God knows how much
a prayer weighs.

MIRACLE FAITH

My family and I took a trip to Maryland and Virginia recently to
visit my mother. On the third night, our oldest son Cade became
sick. He was very, very sick. Just like that our lives began to
change. My wife Chris watched one evening as Cade lost coher-
ence, began to sweat profusely, and decline into a state of despair.
She quickly called our prayer chain to begin to pray. Then we
began to apply the three keys to faith in a very passionate and
immediate way. We learned the value of specific prayer. Here is
the e-mail my wife sent out after the trauma that lasted two plus
days.

> Hi Sharon,
>   I wanted to share the rest of Cade's story with you.
> As you know from my frantic call from Maryland, Cade had
> two doctors diagnose him with spinal meningitis. I imme-
> diately called you to ask for prayer and God began to work
> instantly. Cade had a very high fever, stiff everything, sick
> stomach and photophobic eyes. He suffered from confu-
> sion and was lethargic. As you all started praying, he
> became a bit more aware and able to move a bit easier. By
> the time we got to the ER, the doctor was pleased with his
> ability to move (The doctor from the office also came over
> and noted the improvement). The ER doctor bonded with
> Cade and spent much time with him. I felt like God grant-
> ed us great favor with the doctor and nurses. The doctor
> shared his life story with us and told us we were an encour-
> agement to him! The nurses were very gentle and excellent
> at what they did. God averted a spinal tap (which would

have pushed me over the edge) and Cade went through a scary, but painless CAT Scan. Everything checked out and Cade continued to improve. We were able to leave the hospital that night!

I write this because people tend to ask, "So what caused it?" The answer is simple. Cade had meningitis and God healed him! I have worked in the hospital for years and have seen misdiagnoses. The tendency is to just say 'They don't know' or 'some weird virus.' I must admit that I fell into that mindset. I thanked God for Cade being okay. Not for the healing.

God set the record straight!!!!

Yesterday I received a postcard from a church in Arizona that I visited over 1 year ago. The postcard, which was mailed to my old house and then fowarded on to my current address, said something like this:

'Viral Meningitis is currently rampant in Maricopa County. Please watch your child for any of these symptoms . . .[Cade had all of them]. The incubation period is usually one to three weeks from exposure. If your child exhibits any symptoms get to the doctor immediately!'

If you count back about three weeks, we were in Maricopa County while waiting to get into our new house!!!! I had chills all over as I read the postcard. I felt like God was saying, **"Don't write off my miracle for Cade and you and all who prayed; I did the healing, I get the glory!"** I often pray for God to show me how to love Him the way He deserves to be loved, I feel like this was one of my lessons!

I write this to you because you started the prayer chain and I want everyone to know that God honored those prayers! **Thank you all and ALL GLORY TO GOD!**

Joyfully His, Chris

Agape Papa

The girl was growing weary. Again. Darkness descended in a thud. She could no longer read. Her vision was blurred. Life can be a lot like how she was feeling she thought. She hoped for a light, or did she pray? Just then a light directly over her head flickered on and off giving her a little headache. In perseverance, the little light that could, stayed on, faithful as her companion while she continued her travels through her grandfather's spiritual journal.

It seemed a little odd reading about life from her grandfather's point of view long after he had gone to be with Jesus. Still, his insights did help her see that everyone struggles with the same issues. In the next chapter the young woman would read more from the gospel or good news of her grandfather's life. She would discover it is God who will lift us up.

FAITH FACTOR FOUR

Faith Factor Four states that you have to ask to get the blessing. Faith is a verb. Sometimes we are required to A.S.K. That is we need to keep asking, seeking, and knocking until God's timing and circumstances converge in an answered prayer.

FAITH FACTOR FOUR IN ACTION

Jabez had a hope. *1 Chronicles 4:9-10* We are commanded to love God and others (Deut 6:4-5). And Nehemiah had a burden. *Nehemiah 1-2* What about you? What keeps you up at night? What makes your heart race? What do you dream about? Are you ASKing God about it?

FAITH FACTOR FIVE

God Will Lift You Up:
Three Voices of Faith

Beloved,

"But those who wait on the Lord shall renew their strength; They shall mount up with wings like eagles, they shall run and not be weary, they shall walk and not faint." **Isaiah 40:31**

My youngest son, Cana, was three. He was riding his tricycle up and down a very small street. His mobility to turn was very limited. His tenacity and persistence were unmatched. I watched him pedal, turn, and pedal again. I thought about my ability to focus absolutely on something just like Cana was doing.

I also noticed that as I called to him, he would stop, listen, and obey. Then, moments later, he would go do the exact opposite thing I had asked him to do. It occurred to me that he was hearing "multiple voices." That is, there were competing stimuli moving him toward or away from what was right in front of him. As I watched him in more detail, I could see the spiritual battle for my son. I considered the three voices you and I often respond to. These voices are from God, our own flesh, and the devil.

GOD'S VOICE

I realized that too often in life people, myself included, end up just going through the motions. We can work hard and fast through the initial employment term, school semester, or ministry experience.

Then we settle onto a mindset of the path of least resistance. I watched Cana try with every ounce of effort to pedal, turn, and pedal. He was a whirlwind of activity. He was deeply focused and committed to what he was doing.

I remember how in times past I too could be laser focused and was thrilled to be completely committed to a cause. I recalled the way time could stand still for those who are sold out to a cause. I regretted the time lost and wasted on efforts of mine that were less than all God would have hoped for.

I also noted, as I watched Cana go back and forth, back and forth, that often when I was thoroughly motivated toward the accomplishing of one goal, good things would come my way. When I was in "the zone" and walking by faith, miracles would happen to me. Miracles are not things we can plan for, unless of course we have faith in our heavenly father and His promise to care for our every need. Cana was in a great place as he pedaled back and forth, back and forth.

In this case, God's voice was of protection and comfort and fun. Practically speaking, I was God's instrument of safety. God's voice is peaceable, gentle, willing to yield, full of good fruit and mercy without hypocrisy. His voice is often still and always trusting.

In his determination to grow in his new skill of peddling his tricycle, Cana had moved beyond the protective cocoon of my immediate presence. He had ridden his trike from our narrow little strip of sidewalk over a grassy area and out to a curb. Beyond the curb were onrushing cars. Cars were deadly for a three-year-old on a trike. Though Cana's commitment was commendable, his judgment was suspect. In our own lives, we can be so wrapped up in contingency plans and what if's, that we become paralyzed. This paralysis not only immobilizes our efforts, but it can destroy our faith. When our faith is attacked, we are subject to hopelessness, anger, and often worse. The peaceful voice of God can be lost in our own selfish pursuits.

THE FLESH'S VOICE

The voice of our own flesh can be our own worst enemy. Our voices cry out "ME," "MINE," "MY," and "I." Our voices are self-focused. They are greedy and lament, "I want, I want, I want."

Instead, our lives must reflect a complete trust in God our father. We must be passionate about what is before us. Likewise, we must move forward and explore new areas to grow in our lives. As we live a sold-out life in love with God and what He has put before us, we begin to live a supernatural life.

What happened next to my son Cana would, for his little mind, seem like a supernatural occurrence. I noticed he had scooted precariously near the curb and oncoming traffic. I saw his intent was to expand his riding area. I also saw his life would be terribly short if I didn't intercede. So...

I came upon Cana who was in full pedal toward the intersection. I reached down, grabbed the seat and handle bars of his trike and simply lifted him up off the pavement. I held him closely to my chest. His legs never stopped pedaling through the air. His eyes never wavered on his goal to cross the street. But now he was safe in the arms of his father.

THE DEVIL'S VOICE

The third voice is that of the devil. The devil whispers the D's of the devil into our ears and hearts. Doubt, despair, depression, despondency, decay, distraction, dissatisfaction, delay and ultimately death are the calling cards of the devil. The devil has designs to deliver us incapacitated into eternity. He is the destroyer.

CHILDLIKE FAITH

I love Cana. God loves us. I saw Cana working hard for his goal. His passion placed him in harm's way. My love for him prompted me to protect yet encourage Cana in the pursuit of his goal. Consider: God wants to do the same in your life. In fact, He already may have blessed your life in this way. It could be that you are experiencing His love and protective perspective in your life even now.

In time, I walked Cana safely across the street. I placed him down on the pavement. His legs, peddling the entire time, provided a quick burst of speed and off he went. Safely, Cana peddled into a park area with swings, slides and jungle gyms. He was laughing and giggling the whole time.

I smiled too. It made me happy to protect and help Cana grow in his new skill. I thought of all the spiritual lessons I learned that day. It dawned on me that we need to be committed to what God has placed before us. We should be passionate about our call in life.

Likewise, I sensed that, no matter what, we should always keep peddling. Cana never stopped peddling when I picked him up. We should also delight ourselves in the Lord. As we do this, He will give us the desires of our hearts. *Psalms 32:11* I realized that like myself with Cana, when push comes to shove, God will lift us up. *"But those who wait on the Lord shall renew their strength; They shall mount up with wings like eagles, they shall run and not be weary, they shall walk and not faint."* **Isaiah 40:31**

Here is a lovely poem many are familiar with that illustrates God's care for us as He lifts us up.

One night a man had a dream. He dreamed he was walking along the beach with the Lord. Across the sky flashed scenes from his life. For each scene he noticed two sets of footprints in the sand: one belonging to him and the other to the Lord.

When the last scene of his life flashed before him, he looked back at the footprints in the sand. He noticed many times along the path of life there was only one set of footprints. He also noticed that it happened at the very lowest and saddest times in his life.

This really bothered him, and he questioned the Lord about it. "Lord, You said that once I decided to follow You, You'd walk with me all the way. But I have noticed that during the most troublesome times in my life there was only one set of footprints. I don't understand why, when I needed you most, You would leave me."

The Lord replied, "My son, My precious child, I love you and would never leave you. During your times of trial and suffering when you see only one set of footprints, it was then that I carried you."

Anonymous

THREE VOICES OF FAITH

Here are the three voices of faith:

1. God's voice comes as a still small voice. *James 3:17* tells us God's *"wisdom that is from above is first pure, then peaceable, gentle, willing to yield, full of mercy and good fruits, without partiality and without hypocrisy."*

2. Our own voice of the flesh cries out "ME," "MINE," "MY," AND "I." It asks "what about me?" our voices shout that "my rights are being infringed on here! I am the best, most important, or should get the most credit." Our voices scream, "I did it!" Our voices are offensive to others and bring the stench of pride with them.

3. The third voice of faith is that of the devil. The devil's primary
    aim is to thwart the plans of God. Anything beginning with the
    letter *d* that causes a problem may well be the devil interfering.
    Here are a few examples:

> "I can't do that!" (Doubt)
> "I am so unhappy." (Despair)
> "I'll get to that tomorrow." (Delay)
> "I am so tired, and overwhelmed." (Depression)
> "I just want to give up." (Defeat)
> "I haven't even worked on that for years, just let it go." (Delay)
> "I want to kill myself." (Death-suicide)
> "My dreams are dead; I don't have anything left." (Death of Dreams)
> "If I am with him/her just tonight, no one will know." (Decadence)
> "What? I'm not buzzed!" (Drunkenness)

Can you identify the three voices affecting faith in your life today?
You need to, because your life may be depending on it.

Amanda heard God's voice. He told her how beautiful she was. He
told her she had a bright future. He shared His love with her over
and over. The preacher finished his sermon and Amanda sat
straight up in her chair, ready to respond and come up to the altar
and start over again.

The preacher extended the invitation and just as Amanda prepared
to stand up, a voice in her head interrupted God's soft voice of invitation for peace and hope. In a low repetitious manner she heard
the following words: "Dumb...dumb...dumb...don't be dumb."
The devil had entered the conversation and used the fear of her
youth to halt her progress toward God and the bright future He had
for her.
Next, Amanda began like Eve before her to talk or more accurately "reason" with the devil. Soon even her own flesh would betray
her. "Dumb?" Amanda thought. If I go up there I will look like a

fool, and I can't afford that after all I have been through. My life is worth more than this type of colossal embarrassment. This is really all about ME and besides if I did go up front, I would need someone special to attend to MY needs and right now I don't see anyone special enough for ME.

In that simple little plastic seat at the end of church service a mortal battle ensued. Amanda heard God's voice. She welcomed His warm peaceful embrace. The devil planted seeds of doubt. Her fleshly voice betrayed her own prideful needs. That day Amanda failed to obey God's voice. Amanda stayed in her seat.

Amanda missed church the next week. She would go another time (DELAY). Amanda went out with friends that weekend for a good time (DECADENCE). She had sex with her boyfriend (DEBAUCHERY). The boyfriend beat her silly (DESPAIR). Her friend who took her to church was killed that weekend driving Amanda's car (DEATH). They had decided after Amanda talked everyone into it that they would skip church this week and just go "have some fun."

There are three voices of faith. Which voice are you obeying?

In considering the three voices of faith, one must also note that often God will not always tell us exactly what to do. When this happens, the voice of the flesh and that of the devil can seem overwhelming. What are we to do then?

Many people are stigmatized by the idea of even being able to know God's will for their lives. Questions flood one's mind, questions such as "can I have my own hopes, dreams, desires or burdens?" Also, "how can I be sure that what I want or am thinking is God's will for me?" Other questions come too: Is faith reactive in that I just wait for God to speak to me or can it also be proactive? Is it possible to move in a direction by faith without hearing God distinctly and still be in God's will? If I trust in God's Word, His character, and Son Jesus, am I free to move in areas by faith and expect a blessing or will it end in a curse?

The short answer is "yes you can and should have hopes, dreams, desires and burdens." If you are a Christian, the Holy Spirit lives in you and is guiding, counseling, and directing you. Do not be ashamed of the aspirations of your heart. Faith can be like rocks in a river. To cross over, we need to look at the rocks, step onto the rocks, rest our weight on the rocks as the stream rushes past, balance ourselves on the rocks, and repeat often if we wish to cross the river. The key to discerning which rocks or dreams and desires are for us is a careful, prayerful, step-by-step approach. It is a stepping stone faith.

FLEXIBLE FAITH

Faith can be reactive as David the shepherd boy shows us. In killing a lion and a bear to protect the sheep which God had given him charge over, David reacted to the threat with his experience, skill, and courage. David had a relationship with God but most likely did not spend a whole lot of time in prayer as the impending attacks came upon him and his sheep suddenly.

Faith can also be proactive. Later in David's life he heard about a giant threatening his nation. Giants for us can be symbolic of problems, such as sickness, financial challenge, job loss, marital failings and more. David relied on God's Word (that Israel was God's chosen people). David also relied on God's character trait of faithfulness, which David had seen demonstrated in his experience with the lion and bear. David also trusted that the God who helped him protect a small flock of sheep would be the same God to help him protect a larger flock of people—the very nation of Israel.
Please know this: as we are faithful in the small things, God will give us charge over more. **Matthew 25:23** says, *"well done good*

and faithful servant: you have been faithful over a few things; I will make you ruler over many things. Enter into the joy of the Lord."

Agape Papa

Her grandfather's faith seemed to relax with each passing chapter. She noted that faith can be and should be as effortless as breathing. The girl pondered that unless someone asks us to focus on our breathing patterns, most of the time we never give breathing a thought. Yet breathing is the very source of our lives. She mused. Living a life by faith can be as effortless as breathing. She wanted to experience this. The lovely girl couldn't wait to discover in the next chapter the three cycles of faith that lead to this effortless faith life!

FAITH FACTOR FIVE

Faith Factor Five gives hope that God will lift you up. Faith Factor Five identifies three voices of faith. The voices are God's, the devil's and our own flesh's.

FAITH FACTOR FIVE IN ACTION

Will you commit to listen and obey God's voice this week? It could mean the difference between life and death. Share one scenario in which you will commit right now to listen and obey God's voice.

The WOW Factor:
Three Cycles of Faith

Beloved,

"I love all who...." **Proverbs 8:17-21**

My e-mail friend Bob Johnson passed this story along. It made me say WOW!

John Blanchard stood up from the bench, straightened his Army uniform, and studied the crowd of people making their way through Grand Central Station. He looked for the girl whose heart he knew, but whose face he didn't, the girl with the rose.

His interest in her had begun thirteen months before in a Florida library. Taking a book off the shelf, he found himself intrigued, not with the words of the book, but with the notes penciled in the margin. The soft handwriting reflected a thoughtful soul and insightful mind. In the front of the book he discovered the previous owner's name: Miss Hollis Maynell.

In time and with effort he located her address. She lived in New York City. He wrote her a letter introducing himself and inviting her to correspond. The next day he was shipped overseas for service in World War II.

During the next thirteen months the two grew to know each other through the mail. Each letter was a seed falling on a fertile heart. A romance was budding. Blanchard requested a photograph, but she refused. She felt that if he really cared, it wouldn't matter what she looked like.

When the day finally came for him to return from Europe, they scheduled their first meeting at 7:00 p.m. at Grand Central Station in New York. 'You'll recognize me,' she wrote, 'by the red rose I'll be wearing on my lapel.' So at 7:00 p.m., he was in the station looking for a girl whose heart he loved, but whose face he had never seen. Here is what Mr. Blanchard experienced:

A young woman was coming toward him, her figure long and slim. Her blonde hair lay back in curls from her delicate ears; her eyes were blue as flowers. Her lips and chin had a gentle firmness, and in her pale green suit she was like springtime come alive. He started toward her, entirely forgetting to notice that she was not wearing a rose. As he moved, a small, provocative smile curved her lips.

"Going my way, sailor?" she murmured. Almost uncontrollably, he made one step closer to her, and then he saw Miss Hollis Maynell. She was standing almost directly behind the girl. A woman well past 40, she had graying hair tucked under a worn hat. She was more than plump, her thick-ankled feet thrust into low-heeled shoes. The girl in the green suit was walking away quickly. Mr. Blanchard felt as though he was split in two, so keen was his desire to follow her, and yet so deep was his longing for the woman whose spirit had truly companioned his own. And there she stood.

Her pale, plump face was gentle and sensible; her gray eyes had a warm and kindly twinkle.

Mr. Blanchard did not hesitate. His fingers gripped the small worn blue leather copy of the book that was to identify him to her. This would not be love, but it would be something precious, something even better than love, a friendship for which he had been and must ever be grateful. Mr. Blanchard squared his shoulders, saluted and held out the book to the woman, even though while he spoke he felt choked by the bitterness of his disappointment.

"I'm Lieutenant John Blanchard, and you must be Miss Maynell. I am so glad to meet you; may I take you to dinner?" The woman's face broadened into a tolerant smile. "I don't know what this is about, son,' she answered, 'but the young lady in the green suit who just went by, she begged me to wear this rose on my coat. And she said if you were to ask me out to dinner, I should tell you that she is waiting for you in the big restaurant across the street. She said this was some kind of test!"

It's not difficult to understand and admire Miss Maynell's wisdom. The true nature of the heart is seen in its response to the unattractive. *"Tell me whom you love,"* Houssaye wrote, *"and I will tell you who you are."*

THE WOW FACTOR!

The WOW Factor! had its origin in an idea introduced by Miles McPherson during a faith series preached at the Rock Church in San Diego, California.

The WOW Factor! includes three core tenets: Walk with God, Obey God, and Wait and Watch for God to move in your life. The Bible tells us ". . .*to obey is better than sacrifice.*" **I Samuel 15:22** It is true. If we are faithful to obey God, our lives become blessed in ways we can't imagine. In some cases, God's blessings come as life's little lessons disguised by his wonderful sense of humor. Let me illustrate.

WALK WITH GOD

One night while we were hosting a home Bible study, we witnessed God's flavorful humor in the context of our three-year-old son Cana's potty training.   As the Bible Study progressed, we were walking with God and were diligently studying God's call for each of us to be obedient to His voice. We talked about prayer, the Bible, godly counsel and waiting to hear God's voice. We all nodded our heads in agreement. The lesson still seemed hollow though. That is, until Cana came scampering into the room, his voice at a high squeal.

Allow me to give a little background. My wife and I had been praying to the Lord to help us potty-train Cana. Since he was three, it was time to begin the reward system. It took a few days but Cana began to see the wisdom of our little reward system. We began to see immediate progress.

The deal was a simple one. Any time Cana had to go to the bathroom, he had to tell us. We would walk him to the little potty and sit and read to him as he did his business. If he went pee pee, he would get a piece of candy. If he went poo poo, he would earn a piece of gum. In Cana's world, gum was better because it lasted longer and if he tired of it, it could stick to things very easily. Cana loved walking with his father to the potty.

OBEY GOD

So on this evening, Cana provided the illustration for our study on obedience and God's blessings. We had obeyed God in training our son. Now we wondered if he would obey our words. During the

Bible study we had been looking at the lives of Noah, Abraham, and David. We noted each man was given a promise for his life. We discussed each man's testing of faith. We recognized each man's need to be obedient to God in the midst of great challenge to eventually secure the promised blessing.

Noah was required to build an ark at a time when no boat of any kind existed. He was required to prepare in great detail this ark for a flood that no one had ever experienced before. He was told to bring two of every animal onto his ark. Surely his experience must have told him the danger of lions in a small space. He had to be concerned that tigers would eat the cows at their first opportunity.

Still, Noah persevered in obedience to building the ark for God. The flood did come and the earth as he knew it vanished. All the people who had mocked and ridiculed him were gone. The familiarity of life as he knew it was now radically altered. Noah had obeyed God at a cost of everything familiar and comfortable for him and his family.

Abraham was promised a child to multiply his seed to equal the number of stars in the sky. He laughed at God's first announcement of this blessing. Later, he connived with his wife to make it happen sooner than God had planned. The result was a tragic legacy of strife, enmity, and bitterness in his family and in the nation to come. In time, God fulfilled the promise to Abraham in spite of his partial obedience.

David was anointed by God at a very early age. He had to grow through challenging the giant in his life, Goliath, and gaining victory in the Lord's strength. Later, he soothed King Saul only to be turned on and hunted by the very king he had served. In time, David waited and allowed God to open the throne of the kingdom to David. David's obedience to God was rewarded richly even though later David would commit grievous sin against God.

In our lives, we too can practice obedience. Obedience requires a willing heart. It is reflected in a patient spirit. Obedience is covered by prayer, by a reliance on scripture, and by faith in the one who had given the promise. Obedience is its own reward. Obedience will take us into new areas we are unfamiliar with and require us to wait. Noah's ark, Rahab waiting in her home on the wall, and Abraham's child even when Abraham was at a very old age, are all examples of this new territory faith leads to. In waiting for God to bring about His promise for our lives, we become more dependent on Him. We can also end up separated from the people and things we love and are familiar with. Obedience also is a process of blessing for us.

As we obey God, we choose to do something by faith. It is by faith that we please God. Likewise, our dependence on God grows since our obedience requires us to do something we are not expert at doing. Obedience allows us the privilege of being vulnerable before God. Obedience brings God's grace and mercy directly into our lives. Obedience is the birthing of blessing in each of our lives.

On the evening of our Home Bible Study, Cana provided the illustration for our lesson on obedience. Earlier, he had requested my wife's presence on the "throne." Cana had to go potty. After his initial request and my wife's prompt response (I was leading the study and unfortunately could not attend Cana's necessary needs at this time), our study resumed its original air of casual seriousness. We were deep in scripture after all. We were waiting and watching for God to move in our lives.

WATCH AND WAIT FOR GOD TO MOVE

Ten minutes or so passed and we heard a squeal, a squeak, and great laughter. Next, we heard, "Daddy! Daddy! Daddy!" I turned my head along with the others just in time to see Cana lunge forward and latch onto my neck. His shirt was flapping like old glory. His bottom was as bare as the day he was born.

Cana hugged me, kissed me, completely unaware of the room filled with folks smiling and watching his gleeful interruption. "Daddy! Daddy!" Cana continued. "Two poops in the potty, two poops in the potty," he explained. Next, he danced away from me, lifted both hands high in the air and shouted, "Two poops and a piece of gum! Two poops and a piece of gum." His joy was nearly complete.

Cana was being trained by my wife and I to use his little potty in the bathroom. He was asked to obey our request. We had given him a promise. Naturally, each time he obeyed, he received the blessing. This night was no exception.

First, as we walk with God, God wants to train us. He has asked, is asking, and will ask you and me to obey Him in something specific that He places before us. He will give you and me a promise.

Second, as we obey, good things happen. Like Cana, when we obey, we will receive the blessing. No exceptions.

Third, as we watch for God to move, we will always be pleasantly surprised. I stopped the Bible Study and picked Cana up, put pants on his shiny behind, and gave him a piece of gum. I kissed Cana, again, and sat him on the floor and watched him dance back up the stairs to play with his visiting friends. Cana's joy was complete in his obedience to his parents' request. Life could not have been any better for Cana at that time. Two poops and a piece of gum was the real life illustration God gave us that evening. He wanted us to understand, really understand, the fact that His requests in our lives require obedience. Obedience is a choice. The fruit of obedience is blessing.

Complete obedience in the details of life will bear world-changing fruit just as Noah's obedience saved the world. Partial obedience will bring both a blessing and a curse. Abraham and Hagar are examples of this. Disobedience brings a curse and death of God's promise. David's disobedience disqualified him from building God's temple.

Today, you and I can choose obedience. Complete, total obedience. In choosing obedience, like Cana, we can get victory in an area of our lives that has been messy and stinky. We can experience the sheer joy of dancing in our father's lap rejoicing in our victory of obedience. Lastly, we can enjoy the fruit of blessing from the promise He has given us. Today, we can choose obedience. Today we can grow and be blessed by our heavenly Father. Today, let's choose to obey. Let's choose the WOW Factor! in our lives for once.

Here is the WOW Factor! with three cycles of faith:
1. Walk with God
2. Obey God
3. Wait and Watch for God's provision

THE WOW FACTOR! LIFE

The following story is one of my favorites of all time. I believe it best exemplifies the WOW Factor! working in someone's life. It is the story of *William Borden*. This one came from his book *The Life of William Borden*.

William Borden was born into privilege. His was a life of grand opportunity and wealth beyond imagination. He lived during the end of the colonial era. He lived during a time of increasing missionary revival. He died at age 25 in 1912. Some would argue his life ended too soon; others would say it didn't amount to much.

William, under the influence of his mother, became a Christian at an early age. He was strongly impacted by D.L. Moody among others. William was a bold witness for Christ at the Hill School and later Princeton University.

This was his Walk with God. In spite of classmates' scorn and the lack of approval of leading faculty, William walked with God. He would write in the back of his Bible, 'NO RETREAT.'

Later, despite pleas from others for him to go into the family business, to 'make something of himself,' William stayed true to God's call on his life. He would choose to obey the vision to go to China in order to live with and witness to the Muslim Chinese. In Kansu, Islam, bigoted idolatry, and explosive political worlds collided in a desperate tug of war. To go to China, William would have to give up his life of privilege and possibly lose his worldly inheritance. William chose to obey God and go to China nonetheless. Under NO RETREAT he would write in the back of his Bible, NO RESERVES.

William became very sick on the ship from the United States over to China. He had contracted cerebral meningitis and died shortly thereafter. He had never set foot in China. He had yet to witness or minister to a Chinese person in his new call. To the world, his life seemed a complete gamble that failed. William waited for God to deliver him and watched in faith for it to be so.

Prior to dying, William got his old Bible out and under NO RETREAT and NO RESERVES he wrote, NO REGRETS. William died. It seemed God had truly forgotten His faithful servant. To die at such a young age without ever impacting such a needy country as China seemed a waste. Was this the best ending God could have orchestrated for William's life?

In matters of faith rarely do we understand the impact of one life in the scope of God's plan for mankind. In the case of William Borden, his life, in terms of years lived and people impacted, does seem shortened. Though his philanthropic giving was notable, upon his death we are still left with the sense something was left on the table. Something more was to be done, yet left unfinished. That is until you look back almost 90 years and view his life from the power of his testimony.

You see his life has been shared with countless thousands over the last 90 years or so. Many people have been profoundly impacted for the gospel of Jesus Christ because of Borden's life story. In the Bible there are written four gospels—Matthew, Mark, Luke and John. There is a fifth gospel written as well; it is not in the Bible, and you are writing it. It is the gospel of YOUR life by faith in Jesus Christ. The gospel or "Good News" of William Borden's life has stood the test of time. It continues to impact many lives for Christ. It impacted mine and now I am sharing it with you.

What will you do with the example of the life of William Borden? What will you do with the life given you? It is time for you and me, like Borden, to live a life whose testimony for future generations is NO RETREAT, NO RESERVES, NO REGRETS. When people look at our lives of faith, they will be tempted to shout WOW!

Agape Papa

The splendid orchids of youth had often been told that all one needed was to have faith as a mustard seed and God would meet their faith. She was beginning to get her own insights from her grandfather's writings. One of those insights would say that mustard seed faith, though small, moved the heart of God because it was PURE mustard seed. It is often the purity, not the size, of a person's faith that pleases God. The young lady was being transformed by the writing of a man she hardly knew.

She had often heard that her grandfather would say we have an enemy who wishes to diminish even our purest mustard seed faith.

In delicately unfolding the next brittle and yellow stained page, she was surprised to find who that enemy really is. She noted with urgency the need to be alert as the enemy within lies just around the corner. Something inside her was hopeful and yet sad.

FAITH FACTOR SIX

Faith Factor Six introduces The WOW Factor! Faith Factor Six tells us there are three cycles of faith. They are to Walk with God, Obey God, and Wait for God while Watching for His provision in your life.

FAITH FACTOR SIX IN ACTION

Which of the three cycles of faith do you have the greatest trouble with? Why? Commit to improve in one cycle of faith this week. What does that mean to you? How will you improve in this area? Don't give up! Don't lose hope! God has an answer right around the corner. Rejoice and be prepared to share God's faithfulness in your life.

FAITH FACTOR SEVEN

The Enemy Within:
Three Enemies of Faith

Beloved,

Sadness will come your way. Trust God still.

"This is Carter. Harold's dead." Click. The answering machine recorded the words that would change our lives. That night my mother living in Maryland called to alert us that her husband, Harold, my stepfather, went upstairs to vacuum a room and within five minutes fell with a thump and died of a massive heart attack at the tender age of 54. Within four months, my family and I left our ministry, joined another ministry, and moved from California to Maryland to be with my Mom.

Once we moved to Salisbury, Maryland, our plan was to rent a house for two to three months, then buy a house and settle into our new home, position, and friends. Everything seemed to be falling into place. The very first home we looked at was perfect. We should have bought it. However....

I started to think about things from a selfish point of view. I prayed less, I calculated more. Like Peter, I began to focus on the waves around me instead of the person of Jesus who was calling and providing for me. I ran straight into the three enemies of faith.

ENEMIES OF FAITH

First, I fell into fear. Fear immediately considers the worst-case scenario. In planning, taking note of the "worst case" is a reasonable approach. However, once fear and "worst-case" scenario becomes "most likely" scenario, fear chips away at our faith. Fear and faith cannot co-exist.

Second, I began to harbor unbelief. Unbelief shouts "you are not worthy!" Unbelief cackles "God will do it for someone else but not for you...don't forget your sin and the things you are so unfaithful in." Unbelief also hints that "You failed in something similar to this before and will probably fail at this...because you are not worthy."

Third, I became immobilized by indecision. Indecision is the corrupted arbiter between fear and unbelief. Indecision considers fear and notes the worst is now upon us. Indecision sifts over unbelief and recognizes the ashes of faith beneath the embers of an undeserving life. Indecision snorts, "we shall do nothing today; we need more time to figure this out. What is in front of us is too good to be true; therefore we should be very wary of moving forward in faith." Indecision promotes lives that drift, and drift, and drift....

In our housing dilemma what should have been three months or less of renting became two years. We were cramped, paid too much rent, were inconvenienced, and lost stewardship benefits of home ownership. Oh, I also stressed my wife and kids out for no reason. I was in sin. I was suffering from fear and unbelief. I acted in indecision. It was a nightmare to be sure.

Here is what happened in abbreviated form. God showed us our home. It was beautiful, priced right, in a great neighborhood and best of all God showed it to us BEFORE we moved. His provision was better than perfect. We had one small problem—me. I looked the gift of the Lord in the eye, blinked, turned my back on the blessing, and went on a two-year march of futility that I would wish on no one.

We spent almost two years searching in vain for the "perfect property." Naturally, Fear pointed out the "worst case" scenario in each opportunity. Likewise Unbelief made sure we remembered we were "not deserving" of THAT type of blessing. The sad truth is we made many, many offers on homes only to pull out or self-sabotage the deals at the last moment. If you are a realtor, we owe you an apology even if you don't know us. It was a pitiful time.

We hit rock bottom on Mother's day. My wife and I repented, and asked God to give us one more chance. This time if He would give us one more chance we would put an offer in today if He would just tell us where. Fear, Unbelief, and Indecision rode that day in the car with us.

Just one more chance Lord, we prayed. Instantly the Holy Spirit prompted us to return to the street where He had led us to purchase a home two years previously. Praying the whole ride for guidance, we were surprised to see a For Sale sign on the home next to the one we had put an offer on before. We were scared, and thrilled, and scared.

I stopped the car, got out, knocked on the door, and told the owner we wanted to purchase their home. In 30 days, we owned it. It was less money than we would have paid next door. It was bigger, and a year later when we had to sell in anticipation of a new Call from God, it sold in one week for more money than we paid.

The lesson I learned is that in spite of our fear, unbelief, and indecision, God is faithful. I needed to just look at Jesus. As I love

Jesus, *". . . perfect love casts out fear."* ***1 John 4:18*** God loves you and me and has great things planned for us. Our job is to not allow the enemy within to bring the three enemies of faith into our lives.

The three enemies within are these:
1. FEAR—which considers every opportunity from the point of a "worst case scenario."
2. UNBELIEF—which shouts "YOU ARE NOT WORTHY!"
3. INDECISION—which paralyzes with fear and unbelief any good thing God may have for us.

My friend Carly was completely in bondage to all three enemies during a very critical point of decision-making in her life. Like so many of us, Carly was in a relationship where it had come time to fish or cut bait. She and her boyfriend were happy together, seemingly well suited for each other, and had begun to make plans for marriage. That is until the still small voice of God began to probe.

One day as Carly was seriously considering what to do in the relationship, God softly told her, "he's mine, not yours; you're mine and I have something better for you." Carly was scared. Then she became fearful of all she would lose if she gave this boy up. Next she suffered through unbelief noting that a "bird (boy) in the hand was better than two in the bush." Finally, indecision rent her with migraines, sadness, hopelessness and worse. She couldn't make a decision even though she knew she had heard God.

It took enormous faith, the kind of faith that is desperate and delusional for her to simply obey what God had told her to do. Simultaneously, and unknown to Carly, God was moving her future husband in line to meet and fall in love with her in the church they would both attend together. One year later Carly was engaged to the "perfect man." Carly's faith was richly rewarded. Yours will be too when you act in faith.

THE ATTITUDE OF FAITH

The great thing about faith is that it all depends on your attitude and mine. Will you be defeated by disappointment? Will you be the victim or the victor? The Bible says, *"For as a man thinks in his heart, so is he."* **Proverbs 23:7** Check out this story.

A parable is told of a farmer who owned an old mule. The mule fellinto the farmer's well. The farmer heard the mule 'braying' or whatever mules do when they fall into wells. After carefully assessing the situation,although the farmer sympathized with the mule, he decided that neither the mule nor the well was worth the trouble of saving.

Instead he called his neighbors together and told them what had happened...and enlisted them to help haul dirt to bury the old mule in thewell and put him out of his misery.

Initially, the old mule was hysterical! But as the farmer and hisneighbors continued shoveling and the dirt hit the mule's back...a thought struck that old mule. It suddenly dawned on him that every time a shovel load of dirt landed on his back...he should shake it off and step up! This he did blow after blow.

'Shake it off and step up...shake it off and step up...shake it off and stepup!' he repeated to encourage himself. No matter how painful the blows, or how distressing the situation seemed, the old mule fought panic and just kept right on shaking it off and stepping up!

It was not long before the old mule, battered and exhausted, stepped triumphantly over the wall of that well. What seemed like a burial of him actually blessed him...all because of the manner in which he handled his adversity.

That's life! If we face our problems and respond to them positively,and refuse to give in to panic, bitterness or self-pity...the adversitiesthat come along to bury us usually have within them the potential tobenefit and bless us!

Remember forgiveness, faith, prayer, praise, and hope—all areexcellent ways to 'shake it off and step up' out of the wells in whichwe find ourselves!

*One more thing...never be afraid to try something new. Remember, amateurs built the ark. Professionals built the **Titanic**.*

Author Unknown

In the Christian life there will always be critics. Generally, these critics will have a *" . . . form of godliness but denying its power. And from such people turn away."* **2 Timothy 2:5** In a spiritual sense, we must understand it is the enemy, the great deceiver, Satan himself, who is behind the critical spirit. The reason for the criticism varies depending on the issue at hand.

Suffice it to say, criticism will surface when it is least convenient. Therefore, before the criticism begins, we must prepare our hearts and minds. Prayer, scripture reading, and teaching ourselves and others how to properly handle criticism is critical to diffusing the critical spirit and its cousins gossip, slander, and discord. The primary way we may win the battle against criticism is through a humble and contrite spirit.

Please understand that in most cases the people with the critical spirits simply feel left out. They are generally afraid of the change being contemplated. Their faith is weak or non-existent. They also may be afraid of losing influence or position. The only solution for you and me is to obey God. Love the critics, pray for them, explain once what we feel God telling us to do, and then move on to what is next.

Theodore Roosevelt wrote an essay called *The Man in the Arena*. It provides a clear perspective for those in ministry, for those in the "Arena." He said,

> *It is not the critic who counts, not the one who points out how the strong man stumbled, or how the doer of deeds might have done them better. The credit belongs to the man who is actually in the arena, whose face is marred with sweat and dust and blood...who, if he fails, at least fails while daring greatly, so that his place shall never be with those cold and timid souls, who know neither victory nor defeat.*

SIMPLE FAITH

My daughter Cally is 20 months old. I am not sure why we refer to children's ages in months until about age three but that is the way it is. I always thought it would be fun to tell people I am just about to turn 480 months next week. I don't though. I might seem odd to some folks.

So Cally, who is now 20 months old, has got the hang of this faith stuff. Let me explain. Cally walks around in a world she completely does not understand. There are fearful things all around her like big people, stairs, table corners, and dark rooms. Likewise, she by definition is unqualified for just about anything but a good snuggle and healthy dose of loveage, so her entire life is a life of unbelief. That is, she is not capable of anything other than food, water, a clean diaper, and a good nap. Finally, she is constantly wracked with indecision (should I eat the day old hot dog under my high chair, the week old petrified banana behind the couch, or drink from the toilet again when mommy is not looking?).

How does Cally handle all of this confusion? She handles it like a child. Jesus tells us in **Mark 10:15** *"Assuredly, I say to you, whoever does not receive the kingdom of God as a little child will by no means enter it."* So we can learn a little from Cally.

When she wants something, Cally stands in the middle of whatever room she is in and simply yells "MOMMY" OR "DADA" at the

top of her lungs. If she is fearful, it comes with a cry. If she is feeling unworthy (like when her brothers exclude her from a game) it
comes with a high pitched scream, and when she is undecided, it
comes in a repetitive drone-like "Mommy, mommy, mommy,
mommy, mommy...." You get the drift.

What do you think my wife and I do when she is calling us? Yes,
you guessed it. We come to her. If she is fearful, we pick her up
and love her. If she is suffering from unbelief, we try to correct the
situation with her brothers and make it a bit more equitable. In
times of indecision, we either take a few choices away from her or
take her away from the choices so she can concentrate on the best
choice in front of her. Consider for a moment that God (your
Father) does exactly the same for you and me when we walk by
faith.

Here is a story modified from a Greg Laurie Harvest Crusade
brochure. This story is really compelling and speaks to all three
enemies within converging in a single catastrophic event.

LESSONS FROM THE *TITANIC*

> It was the greatest maritime disaster in human history.
> Some had said of the *Titanic*, 'Even God Himself couldn't
> sink it.' But on April 14, 1912, just five days into its maid-
> en voyage, the *Titanic* went down, taking 1,500 people to an
> icy grave. Countless thousands are hearing this dramatic
> story for the first time through the film *Titanic*. It is now the
> highest box office draw of all time. Many people have gone
> to see it_repeatedly, enthralled by its story, moved by its
> characters. Why has it gripped the world's imagination for
> 85 years?

The Ship of Dreams

Perhaps the story of the *Titanic* looms larger than life because it was a "ship of dreams." This massive ship, the largest and most luxurious of its day, was a grandiose symbol of its time. People held a buoyant optimism about the future. A new philosophy for living was emerging. The new century had just dawned, and man was going to build a "heaven on earth."

The thought prevailed that perhaps mankind could "best nature" and "even God" through technology. As a result, when the *Titanic* was built, nothing was spared. It harnessed all of the latest technology; it was filled with luxurious staterooms and elegant dining halls. And when it was finished, people called it "unsinkable."

The "Millionaire Special"

It seemed that everybody of stature wanted to be a part of its maiden voyage. So many millionaires were on board that it was dubbed, "The Millionaire Special." The combined wealth of its passengers equaled $500 million (multiplied billions in today's economy)!

The ship's passenger list included some of the world's wealthiest people. John Jacob Astor, whose fortune was estimated at $150 million, was returning from a trip to Egypt with his new 19-year-old bride. Benjamin Guggenheim, valued at $95 million, was on board with his mistress. Isadore Strauss, founder of Macy's department store, worth $50 million, secured passage, as did Jay Ismay, with an estimated wealth of $40 million. Today's counterpart would be to set sail on a cruise with Ross Perot, Bill Gates, Steven Forbes, Steven Spielberg, and Donald Trump.

Fear considers every opportunity a worst-case scenario. When fear attaches itself to leadership, it is often accompanied by pride. Pride is the henchman of fear and masks wisdom, sound judgment, and servant-hood with a self-serving arrogance. Typically, the most fearful leaders are also the most proud. This in turn leads to retarded organizations, underachieving teams, and generally poor performance. In some cases it results in death.

"Shut-up, shut-up! We're busy!"

Most of us are familiar with the story of the sinking of this great ship. There were repeated warnings of icebergs ahead. One ship, the *Californian*, sent the message via Morse code, "I say, old man, we are surrounded by ice!"

The reply from the *Titanic* was both tragic and telling. It wired back, "Shut-up, shut-up! We're busy!"

Despite repeated warnings (seven in all), the *Titanic* passed ahead until it hit an iceberg that tore a 200-foot gash in its side. But when the passengers were instructed to get into the lifeboats, they failed to take the danger seriously. Some just went to be cooperative, confident the titanic would be fine. Many of the passengers just laughed it off—drinking, dancing, gambling, and partying the night away. One person grabbed some broken chunks of ice from the iceberg saying, "Get me another one for my drink." Others took hunks of ice back to their staterooms to show their friends when they arrived in New York City.

Still others put their life jackets on and danced around the deck while onlookers laughed. Some refused to put the life jackets on because they didn't want to dirty or wrinkle their expensive clothes.

Unbelief shouts, "you are not worthy" which can result in denial of
fear. Denial as it pertains to unbelief whispers things like "ignore
that idea; it's not for you." Denial also says, "things aren't so bad;
this latest issue will just go away." Denying or refusing to see a
problem is the beginning of the end for any person, team, organi-
zation, or ship.

Room in the Lifeboats

The ship's stewards literally broke into staterooms in order
to rouse people from sleep and warn them of the peril. Most
passengers simply couldn't believe that this unsinkable ship
could actually sink. Because of their unbelief, lifeboat after
lifeboat pulled away from the ship with only 10 to 15 per-
sons on board, though they had a capacity of up to 60.
When a series of loud explosions rocked the ship, it woke
the people to their impeding doom, and panic ensued as
they stampeded toward the remaining lifeboats.

Indecision paralyzes through fear and unbelief. It tortures with
mental turmoil any and every good thing that God may present.
Indecision causes terrible immobility in one's life. It promotes a
lack of any type of decision-making. So the natural cycle of indecision is this: faith, choice, fear, unbelief, and indecision. This cycle
brings great frustration, anger, bitterness, resentment, and eventually apathy into the lives of those poisoned by indecision. It can also
bring death.

Money Can't Buy You Life

There are many ironies associated with this tragedy. Chief among
them was that many of those who perished on the ship could have
"bought" the ship. But their money was not enough to secure just
one seat on a lifeboat.

Imagine those men and women standing on the decks—
some draped in the finest furs that money could buy, others
with rings on their fingers, pearls around their necks, diamond earrings in their ears and diamond tiaras in their hair.
Yet, at that moment, their lives counted for no more or less
than the poorest steerage passenger. One first class passenger, realizing his fate, went to the side of the ship and
dumped out all his money. Through it all, the band played
on until the final horrible end.

The *Titanic*'s Message Today

If there is a message in the sinking of the *Titanic*, it may be that man
has turned a deaf ear to his fate. While the world around us sinks,
we choose to believe that everything is going to be all right. But is
it? Should we party our lives away and forget that something called
death is inevitably coming? It has been said that the statistics on
death are quite impressive—one out of every one person dies.

You may be caught up in pursuing a career right now, chasing that
elusive raise or that valued promotion. You may be hoping that
once you reach that certain plateau, you will finally be "happy."
But will you? What good was all the wealth of those who died that
night in the icy Atlantic? Of what value was all that money when
the ship was sinking?

Life Can be Like the *Titanic*

The *"Titanic"* we've booked passage on can come in the form of
careers, relationships, and even religion. But one day those ships
will sink, and like the passengers aboard the *Titanic*, we will face
eternity. Life for each one of us—whether the most famous person
or the least heard of—must eventually come to an end.

Do not fear! God has provided a lifeboat for you!

God has provided a lifeboat for all of mankind. It is found in a relationship with Him through His Son, Jesus Christ. You see, we are all separated from God by our sin, be it intentional or unintentional. The Bible tells us, *"All have sinned and fallen short of the glory of God. . ."* **Romans 3:23** There is not a single exception to that statement. Every *"Titanic"* will sink!

That is why some two thousand years ago, Jesus Christ the Son of God, died on a cross for our sin. He personally paid the price for the sins we have committed.

Beyond Unbelief!

Jesus said, *"For God so loved the world that He gave His only begotten Son, that whosoever believes in Him [trusts in, clings to, relies on Him] should not perish, but have everlasting life."* **John 3:16** Just as those passengers on the *Titanic* entrusted their lives to a lifeboat to keep them from an icy grave, so, too, we must entrust our lives to the "lifeboat" of Christ.

How to Get on Board . . .

In fact, committing your life to Christ can be compared to being on board the *Titanic.* As the water floods the decks, you realize you have only moments to decide. You can get into a lifeboat and live, or stay on the *Titanic* and die.

Break Through Indecision!

You might say, "I'm undecided! I'll just stay here and think about it for awhile." But to do so means certain death. Either you leave the *Titanic* for the lifeboat, or you stay on board and go down.

The same is true of becoming a Christian. You either are one—or you are not. Jesus has said that we are either for Him or against Him. To be undecided is to be decided—decidedly against Him.

> Do you want to get into God's lifeboat?
> Do you want to be prepared for eternity?
> Do you want to find the meaning and purpose of life?

Do not foolishly say, like those on board that night, "Shut-up, shut-up! We're busy!" Take these steps and secure your passage to eternity!

1.   Realize that you are a sinner. Our sin of fear is overcome by faith in believing we will always "miss the mark" apart from Jesus. No matter how good a life we try to live, we will still fall miserably short of God's standards. Jesus tells us, "*No one is good, but one, that is, God.*" **Matthew 19:17** Another word for "good" is righteous. The word *righteous* means "one who is as he or she ought to be." Apart from Jesus Christ, we cannot become the person we "ought to be."

2.   Recognize that Jesus Christ died on the cross for you. Our sins of unbelief are overcome by faith that Jesus in us is greater than any outside circumstances we may face. Scripture says, "*But God showed His great love for us by sending Christ to die for us while we were still sinners.*" **Romans 5:8** God gave His very Son to die in our place when we least deserved it. As the Apostle Paul said, ". . .[Christ] *loved me and gave Himself for me . . . .*" **Galatians 2:20**

3.   Repent of your sin. Indecision, which combines fear and unbelief, is defeated when we acknowledge our shortcomings. We need to be refreshed in the truth that God's mercies are new every morning for each of us. Believe this and receive it! The Bible tells us to "repent" and be converted. The word "repent" means to change our direction in life. Instead of running from God, we can run toward Him.

Interestingly, it is God who will help us overcome our fear, unbelief, and indecision. The way to overcome fear, unbelief, and indecision is to trust God, not our circumstances. Trusting God can be hard for so many people. If it is hard for you, just imagine yourself as a 20-month-old in the middle of the living room just crying out to God in your LOUD voice. He will hear, and He will respond. God is our good Father.

SOMETHING YOU DID NOT SEE IN THE MOVIE...

There is, finally, another little-known story about that fateful night. After the tragedy, some survivors spoke of an old preacher who had been a passenger on the *Titanic*. As the ship sank, he was thrown into the freezing Atlantic. When he realized he could not save his own life, he swam from lifeboat to lifeboat, raft to raft, piece of ship to piece of ship, crying out to the people, "Trust Christ. Take Him as Savior. Receive Him into your heart. Call upon the name of the Lord and you will be saved."

Agape Papa

The young lady was learning that on the ship of life, God is already speaking. She realized that we don't need to wait for life's icebergs to hit before we trust Him and live by faith. She also realized that when God shows up in people's lives and they understand what needs to be done, they must do it and do it right away. She wanted to reflect on this thought before moving on. She sensed one day it could save her life.

Sitting in an old, smelly, hot and dusty attic, the young girl reflected on just the moment she found herself in. Here she was discovering a treasure of intimate detail about her grandfather. Time had stopped for her hours ago. This journal provided both personal detail and spiritual nourishment. She exhaled for what seemed the first time in hours. Had she been breathing all along? Was this a dream of hers? No matter, she thought, it was time to explore three opportunities for faith next.

FAITH FACTOR SEVEN

Faith Factor Seven shows there are the three enemies of faith that come from within our own minds. They are fear, unbelief, and indecision.

FAITH FACTOR SEVEN IN ACTION

Can you identify fear, unbelief, and indecision in your life? Stop and take time to confess these sins to God. Now, develop a plan to move beyond faithlessness to faith in each of the areas you listed.

FAITH FACTOR EIGHT

The Upside Down Life
Three Opportunities For Faith

My beloved,

Always remember God gets the most.

GOD GETS THE MOST

The upside-down-life rule number one is that **you can't out-give God**. No matter what we give God, so long as it is with a pure heart, we bless Him. Often our smallest gifts are His greatest treasures. This story from Bob Johnson underscores how God delights in our simplest efforts to please Him.

On a special Teachers' Day, a Kindergarten teacher was receiving gifts from her pupils. The florist's son handed her a gift. She shook it, held it overhead, and said, 'I bet I know what it is, some flowers.' 'That's right' the boy replied, 'but how did you know?' 'Oh just a wild guess,' she replied.

The next pupil was the candy store owner's daughter. The teacher held her gift overhead, shook it and said, 'I bet I can guess what this is, a box of candy.' 'That's right but how did you know?' asked the girl. 'Oh just a wild guess,' the teacher said.

The next gift was from the son of a liquor store owner. The teacher held it overhead, but it was leaking. She touched a drop of the leakage with her finger and touched it to her tongue. 'Is it wine?' She asked. 'No,' the boy replied, obviously delighted that he was the first student to defy, at least temporarily, the teacher's apparent insight. The teacher repeated the process, touching another drop of the leakage to her tongue. 'Is it champagne?' she asked. 'No,' the clearly delighted boy answered. Once again the teacher tasted the leakage and finally said, 'I give up, what is it?'

The boy enthusiastically replied, 'It's a puppy!'

Giving should be cheerful. Never give out of guilt. Try to give more than you think you can. God will always come through for you, always.

"'Will a man rob God? Yet you have robbed me!' But you say, 'In what ways have we robbed you?' 'In tithes and offerings. You are cursed with a curse, for you have robbed me, even this whole nation. Bring all the tithes into the storehouse, that there may be food in my house, and try me now in this,' says the Lord of hosts, 'if I will not open for you the windows of heaven and pour out for you such blessing that there will not be room enough to receive it. And I will rebuke the devourer for your sakes, so that he will not destroy the fruit of your ground, nor shall the vine fail to bear fruit for you in the field,' says the Lord of hosts; 'And all nations will call you blessed, for you will be a delightful land,' says the Lord of hosts." **Malachi 3:8-12**

God gets the most. I learned this through a poignant illustration from my six-year-old son Cade. The lesson was so simple that the profound nature of his comments took me by surprise: God gets the most.

On Cade's sixth birthday, one of his gifts was a ten-dollar bill. He was thrilled! In fact, it was his favorite gift. As I watched Cade celebrate his gift of cash, I was more and more taken by his joy over this particular gift. I'm here to say Cade was a blessed man that day.

The day wore on and about every three or four minutes, Cade would pull his ten-dollar bill out of his pocket and just look at it. He would remind us of his ten dollars and show it to us just before he stuffed it back in his pocket. His mind was filled with the possibilities. He was dreaming big dreams.

I noted Cade spent a lot of time thanking us for his ten-dollar bill. I thought of how little I thanked God for gifts He had given me. The more excited Cade got, the more pensive I became. I reflected on the numerous times God had blessed me and yet too often I took it for granted. Cade's focus on God's blessing in his life caused me to rethink my response to what God had done for me in the past as well as what He wanted to do in me today and into the future.

The next thing Cade did completely amazed me. In fact, it stopped me cold in my tracks. I have never had the spiritual emphasis that Cade had that day. I doubt most adult Christians have the focus Cade had. In considering what Cade decided that day, ask yourself, would you have done the same thing? Will you do the same thing?

Here is what Cade did. Sometime later in the afternoon, just prior to dinner, Cade came to his mother and me to let us know that he had decided what he was going to do with his "big money" ten-dollar bill. We all sat down at the kitchen table. I considered what I thought Cade might do with his money. My list went something like this: candy, bubble gum, a slurpee, a pocket knife, candy, chocolate chip cookies, a whiffle bat and ball, candy... well, you get the idea.

Cade had another plan. He told us in a very sincere way that his ten-dollar bill was going to be spent in the following manner. He would give six dollars to God and put three dollars into his checking account so he could pray about how God wanted him to spend it. The last dollar went into his 7-11 fund.

Too often in my life, and perhaps in yours too, we have short-changed God. I have tithed my 10 percent, but that's it. My faith can stretch only so far. Naturally, the 90 percent left over is all mine. I typically managed "my" 90 percent as if God gave me the money, and I no longer needed to ask for His wisdom.

Maybe your view of possessions is that God gave them to you and it is up to you to do with them as you wish. That's what I thought. Until I heard Cade tell his mother and me how he wanted to manage the money God gave him. Until I heard why Cade did what he did!

Once I closed my gaping mouth, I asked Cade the following question. "Why are you giving $6.00 to God?" At first he didn't understand what I was asking, so I rephrased my question. "Cade, why are you giving God so much of your money?"

A light went on in Cade's mind. He frowned with a look of disbelief that said "You can't be asking me **this** question!" Cade sat up, looked my wife and me both in the eyes and explained his decision this way: "God gets the most."

What would you do? I wish I were more spiritual, but after she closed her own gaping mouth, my wife gently reached over and closed my mouth, again. Cade went on to explain to us that since God had given him the ten dollars, it was Cade's responsibility to give most of the money back to God. According to Cade, God had better ideas for using the money than Cade did.

Cade noted that although he was required to tithe ten percent or one dollar of his gift, it was better for him to please God by giving back more than that. I asked him how he was going to spend the three dollars in his checking account. Cade told me he wanted to buy bubble gum and a magnifying glass. However, he wanted to wait and make sure God would bless him if he bought these items.

Soon after his birthday, Cade had a loose tooth. One night at his grandparents' house, his tooth came out. In the morning, he had a note under his pillow. He also had a twenty-dollar bill. His mother and I had nothing to do with that. It dawned on me that God had given Cade more responsibility and a greater blessing since he was faithful to give God the most.

God also invites all of us to test Him. He promises a blessing if we are willing to submit our hearts and desires to Him. If we walk by faith in our finances, God promises to bless us. Cade understood this with his childlike faith. God rewarded him with a 200 percent return on his original cash blessing. Consider your own finances and believe God to be faithful to His word. Test God on this and your life will change forever. Will you allow yourself, by faith, to be vulnerable financially to God?

THE LAST SHALL BE FIRST

The upside-down-life rule number two is that **the last shall be first**. *Matthew 19:30* tells us *"But many who are first will be last, and the last first."* Bob Johnson passed this story to me via the internet. It speaks to the idea that the last will be first.

> Her name was Mrs. Thompson. And as she stood in front of her 5th grade class on the very first day of school, she told the children a lie. Like most teachers, she looked at her students and said that she loved them all the same. But that was impossible, because there in the front row, slumped in his seat, was a little boy named Teddy Stoddard.
> Mrs. Thompson had watched Teddy the year before and noticed that he didn't play well with the other children, that his clothes were messy and that he always needed a bath. And Teddy could be unpleasant. It got to the point where Mrs. Thompson

would actually take delight in marking his papers with a broad red pen, making bold X's and then putting a big "F" at the top of his papers. At the school where Mrs. Thompson taught, she was required to review each child's past records and she put Teddy's off until last. However, when she reviewed his file, she was in for a surprise.

Teddy's first grade teacher wrote, 'Teddy is a bright child with a ready laugh. He does his work neatly and has good manners . . . he is a joy to be around.' His second grade teacher wrote, 'Teddy is an excellent student, well-liked by his classmates, but he is troubled because his mother has a terminal illness and life at home must be a struggle.' His third grade teacher wrote, 'His mother's death has been hard on him. He tries to do his best, but his father doesn't show much interest and his home life will soon affect him if some steps aren't taken.' Teddy's fourth grade teacher wrote, 'Teddy is withdrawn and doesn't show much interest in school. He doesn't have many friends and sometimes sleeps in class.'

By now, Mrs. Thompson realized the problem, and she was ashamed of herself. She felt even worse when her students brought her Christmas presents, wrapped in beautiful ribbons and bright paper, except for Teddy's. His present was clumsily wrapped in the heavy, brown paper that he got from a grocery bag. Mrs. Thompson took pains to open it in the middle of the other presents. Some of the children started to laugh when she found a rhinestone bracelet with some of the stones missing and a bottle that was one quarter full of perfume. But she stifled the children's laughter when she exclaimed how pretty the bracelet was, putting it on, and dabbing some of the perfume on her wrist. Teddy Stoddard stayed after school that day just long enough to say, "Mrs. Thompson, today you smelled just like my Mom used to." After the children left she cried for at least an hour. *On that very day, she quit teaching reading and writing and arithmetic. Instead, she began to teach children.*

Mrs. Thompson paid particular attention to Teddy. As she worked with him, his mind seemed to come alive. The more she encouraged him, the faster he responded. By the end of the year, Teddy had become one of the smartest children in the class and, despite her lie that she would love all the children the same, Teddy became one of her "teacher's pets." A year later, she found a note under her door, from Teddy, telling her that she was the best teacher he had ever had in his whole life.

Six years went by before she got another note from Teddy. He then wrote that he had finished high school, third in his class, and she was still the best teacher he had ever had in his whole life. Four years after that, she got another letter, saying that while things had been tough at times, he'd stayed in school, had stuck with it, and would soon graduate from college with the highest of honors. He assured Mrs. Thompson that she was still the best and favorite teacher he had ever had in his whole life. Then four more years passed and yet another letter came. This time he explained that after he got his bachelor's degree, he decided to go a little further. The letter explained that she was still the best and favorite teacher he had ever had. But now his name was a little longer. The letter was signed, *Theodore F. Stoddard, M.D.*

The story doesn't end there. You see, there was yet another letter that spring. Teddy said he'd met a girl and was going to be married. He explained that his father had died a couple of years ago and he was wondering if Mrs. Thompson might agree to sit in the place at the wedding that was usually reserved for the mother of the groom. Of course, Mrs. Thompson did. And guess what? She wore that bracelet, the one with several rhinestones missing. And she made sure she was wearing the perfume that Teddy remembered his mother wearing on their last Christmas together. They hugged each other, and Dr. Stoddard whispered in Mrs. Thompson's ear, 'Thank you, Mrs. Thompson, for believing in me. Thank you so much for making me feel important and showing me that I could make a difference.'

Mrs. Thompson, with tears in her eyes, whispered back. She said, *"Teddy, you have it all wrong. You were the one who taught me that I could make a difference. I didn't know how to teach until I met you."*

Here is a lesson in God's perspective.

"But now, O Lord, You are our Father; we are the clay, and You our potter; and we all are the work of Your hand." **Isaiah 64:8**

I learned a simple lesson from a daily devotion and my three-year-old son, Cana. The lesson spoke to God's perspective. It reminded me how limited my wisdom really is. It also touched my heart deeply. Let me share it with you.

One morning as I was praying, Cana brought me a daily devotion. More accurately, he plunked a radio on my head as I prayed. I sensed God had used Cana to speak to me that day, so I stopped praying and listened to the following devotion from a "Teachable Moment" radio segment.

A mother sat in a portable chair on her front lawn. On the freshly cut grass in front of her played her only son. He was four years old. He was thin of stature, frail and possessed a horrible hump, a deformity of birth, on his upper back and neck. The mother read her paper as her child played with trucks, trains, and blocks at her feet.

A little neighbor boy came out of his garage chasing an errant ball. As the ball rolled onto the lawn of the mother and her hunchback child, the laughter and squeals of the neighbor boy turned to silence. Cautiously the young boy inched toward his ball. His eyes never left the back of the boy playing at his mother's feet.

The mother paused from reading her paper and quietly, nervously, braced for the inevitable. This mother had witnessed her child being ignored, shunned, teased, misunderstood, ridiculed and worse. The best she knew to do was to sit with her child as he played. She hoped, she prayed, that just her presence would lessen the humiliation and hurt he would suffer each time another child came into his presence.

The neighbor child, also four years old, was not stooped. He slowly got next to the mother's boy. The neighbor boy was quietly looking into her son's eyes while gently touching his truck. They shared a smile. Then, a giggle. The mother continued to tense up.

Then something scary, amazing, and altogether miraculous happened. The little neighbor boy moved from stroking a toy to stroking ever so gently the hump on the little boy's back. The mother gasped, forgot to breathe, and then sat in stunned silence. The neighbor child looked at the child with the hump and asked, 'What is this?' The mother sat in suspended disbelief.

Her son continued playing with his truck and stated in a whisper, 'My hump.'

"What's it for?" the neighbor child asked, smiling and cocking his head nearer his new friend.

The child at his mother's feet had seen this part before. He remained silent. He didn't want to bring any unnecessary embarrassment on his mom. He also didn't want to be hurt anymore himself. So he remained silent, head down, playing with his truck.

"I know what it's for," the neighbor boy persisted.

"What?" the hunched boy responded, amazed that he would ask. Still, he looked down playing with his truck.

"It's your pouch. God gave you a pouch so your wings would be safe so when you get to heaven they will be the biggest wings ever."

Tears streamed down the mother's cheeks. Her son looked up and smiled at his new friend.

The neighbor child grinned and said, "I can't wait to get my wings so I can fly with you."

The mother sat back and let the tears flow. A smile moved to her face.

This mother had experienced God's perspective in the life of her child. This story also helped me to see God's perspective. It helped me to not be so selfish and judgmental. It helped me to see life for a moment through Jesus' eyes. I hope it helped you. I pray others will look at me in mercy with compassion and love. How about you?

You and I also need God's perspective in our lives. When we give God's perspective to others, it gives us a sense of peace and joy. When others reflect God's perspective to us, we feel humility, love, healing, and God's grace and mercy.

What is it in your life today that you need to ask for God's perspective on? Who can you give God's perspective to today?

In our everyday lives, we can spend too much time focused on what we do have and do not have compared to others. Seeing people who have more than we do causes us to covet. Those folks less fortunate can prompt us to pity or judge unfairly. In some cases of disease, deformity, or retardation, we can be cruel, inhospitable, or worse.

Yet Jesus spent time with those who were outcast from society because of disease or worse. *Matthew 8:1-3* tells us,

> *"When he had come down from the mountain, great multitudes followed him. And behold, a leper came and worshiped him, saying, 'Lord, if You are willing, You can make me clean.' Then Jesus put out his hand and touched him, saying, 'I am willing; be cleansed.' Immediately his leprosy was cleansed."*

Jesus, armed with God's perspective, time and again did the thing that reached to the very core of the people, both those He ministered to and those who witnessed his ministry. Are you in need of a supernatural touch from God? Perhaps He wants to use you to minister to an area in someone else's life that speaks of His love, care, concern, and hope for that person. Maybe you need to open up enough today to receive that tender touch from God in your life.

Here are two ethical questions that underscore the rule that the last shall be first. Consider your answers to the following dilemmas.

> Question 1: If you knew a woman who was pregnant, who had 8 kids already— three were deaf, two were blind, one mentally retarded, and she had syphilis—would you recommend that she have an abortion?

Question 2: It is time to elect a world leader, and your vote counts. Here are the facts about the three leading candidates:

Candidate A—He associates with crooked politicians and consults with astrologists. He's had two mistresses. He chain-smokes and has 10 martinis a day.

Candidate B—He was kicked out of office twice, slept until noon, used opium in college, drank a quart of whisky every evening, and smoked ten cigars each day.

Candidate C—He is a decorated war hero. He's a vegetarian, doesn't smoke, drinks an occasional beer and hasn't had any extra-marital affairs, and loves art.

Which of these candidates would be your choice?

Candidate A is Franklin Roosevelt
Candidate B is Winston Churchill
Candidate C is Adolph Hitler

...and by the way: the answer to the abortion question—if you said "yes," you just killed Beethoven!

Indeed God's ways are not our ways especially in the realm of faith. *Isaiah 55:8* says,

"'For my thoughts are not your thoughts, nor are your ways my ways,' says the Lord. 'For as the heavens are higher than the earth, so my ways are higher than your ways, and my thoughts than your thoughts.'"

DEATH BRINGS LIFE

The upside-down-life rule number three is that **death brings life**. This story from Elizabeth Marsh brings the point into focus.

> Many years ago, when I worked as a volunteer at Stanford Hospital, I got to know a little girl named Liz who was suffering from a rare and serious disease. Her only chance of recovery appeared to be a blood transfusion from her 5-year- old brother, who had miraculously survived the same disease and had developed the antibodies needed to combat the illness. The doctor explained the situation to her little brother, and asked the boy if he would be willing to give his blood to his sister. I saw him hesitate for only a moment before taking a deep breath and saying, "Yes I'll do it if it will save Liz." As the transfusion progressed, he lay in bed next to his sister and smiled, as we all did, seeing the color return to her cheeks. Then his face grew pale and his smile faded. He looked up at the doctor and asked with a trembling voice, "Will I start to die right away?" Being young, the boy had misunderstood the doctor. He thought he was going to have to give his sister all of his blood.

> *"But the angel answered and said to the women, 'Do not be afraid, for I know that you seek Jesus who was crucified, He is not here; for He is risen, as He said. Come, see the place where the Lord lay. And go quickly and tell His disciples that He is risen from the dead, and indeed He is going before you into Galilee; there you will see Him. Behold I have told you."* **Matthew 28:5-8**

In this passage we are given clear instruction for bringing life from death. Faith requires us to be very sensitive to our surroundings. God speaks to us several ways, such as through scripture, through impressions when we pray, and through other believers. Likewise, situations and circumstances can also help us understand God's voice in our lives. The angel came first to the women who were the last at the cross and the first to the tomb. Their faithfulness was rewarded with a greater task. They went from worshipping Jesus at the cross to spreading the "Gospel" (Good News) to the disciples at the tomb during the darkest moment in all of their lives. The death of Jesus led to life for the women.

First, like the women at the cross we must COME to the place where we are willing to be used even if it is from a place of intense disappointment. The women had just seen a horrifying crucifixion of their Lord. All hope in the plans for their lives had been lost. Their dreams had surely just died. God's dream for them was just about to come alive. Now by faith they were supposed to believe that a possible hoax was in fact a supernatural event.

Next, SEE for yourself that the Lord is who He says He is in your life and the lives of others. The women had witnessed from Jesus Himself the servant-leader style of living. When it was their turn, they did well to emulate Jesus. Mike Macintosh once shared how D.L. Moody said, "the measure of a man is not how many servants you have but how many men you serve."

Third, we are to GO— that is to move outward from ourselves and share the great things we have seen. In a faith class I have taught, we have three essential assignments. Assignment one is to go in groups of three or four people and share the gospel with someone "on the streets." Assignment two is to feed and clothe someone. Assignment three is to repent, reconcile, and restore a relationship with someone you have been at odds with. This is the idea of Go. Perhaps you might consider doing each of these assignments by faith too.

Finally, we are told to TELL others. The life of faith in one person's life can radically alter the lives of others willing to be inspired

and used by God to help bring life from death. When we share stories of faith with each other, we encourage one another and we
expand the kingdom. George Mueller was a man of faith. He
prayed and God answered his prayers. The following example
from the book *George Mueller: Man of Faith* shows how a simple
idea can bring life out of death for people in desperate need.

> Mueller had a sense God had called him to start an
> orphanage. He had prayed for a long time about the orphan-
> age. Children were dying on the streets; was there some
> way he could do something to help them? One day God
> told him to stop thinking about it and do it. After Mueller
> obeyed, God gave him the facility, then the beds, then the
> tables, then the food, and so much more. God gave Mueller
> all he asked for. The day to open up arrived, but something
> was missing. Mueller had forgotten to pray for the children.
> Straightaway he corrected his error, prayed for children to
> come, and in time his orphanages became the talk of the
> community and eventually the world.

What would have happened if Mueller had ignored God's call to
start the orphanage? How many lives, eventually saved from physical death as well as eternal damnation, would have been lost had
Mueller not taken God at His word and started the orphanages by
faith? What is God challenging you to do? Do not be concerned if
you have missed opportunities in the past. Instead *"Trust in the
Lord with all of your heart and lean not on your own understanding, and in all your ways acknowledge Him and He will make your
paths straight."* **Proverbs 3:5**

Do not be ashamed or disheartened if you sense missed opportunities in your life. Remember God is in the business of bringing life
out of death. This includes obedience from our disobedience, faith
from our fears and blessings from trials.

Agape Papa

Her grandfather certainly had an active faith life the girl noted. It made her consider what her own faith life looked like. That is how it would look if she decided to begin writing about the faith walk her life was going to represent. She wondered why more people didn't do this type of thing. She thought how sad it would have been had he not written his life of faith down.

Though tired and parched for thirst, she kept plugging away at the journal. She was near the end of the writing and wanted to get the full picture of what was being said. She sensed her grandfather was saying to keep an eye out because just around the corner are three outcomes of faith. She could feel his writings now. To her his next point was to warn us to make sure we don't leave unopened a gift God has given us. It may have a pleasant surprise inside.

FAITH FACTOR EIGHT

In Faith Factor Eight we are told that the upside-down life offers many opportunities for faith. Three opportunities for faith include these: you can never out-give God, if you want to lead you must serve, and death brings life.

FAITH FACTOR EIGHT IN ACTION

Have you ever been afraid to tithe? Have you made excuses about serving someone or someplace that seemed "beneath" your abilities or qualifications? Are you fearful of allowing a dream, hope, relationship or other opportunity the chance to die? It is time to take God at His word. Name one thing in your life that you will submit to God as an opportunity for faith to be released in your life.

FAITH FACTOR NINE

A Gift Unopened
Three Outcomes of Faith

Beloved,

Be mindful of a gift unopened in your life.

"Joseph went out from Galilee...to be registered with Mary, his betrothed wife, who was with child. So it was, while they were there, the days were completed for her to be delivered. And she brought forth her first born son, and wrapped Him in swaddling clothes, and laid Him in a manger, because there was no room for them in the inn." **Luke 2:5-7**

OUR HOPE FULFILLED

This is the story of a gift unopened and how we can miss good things in our lives if we are not careful. We can miss our hope being fulfilled, our faith being increased, and the opportunity to use our lives as a testimony for God's glory and greater opportunities.

I came home one day shortly after the Christmas holiday. Six days after Christmas to be exact. I had wondered when my boys were going to open a very tall gift that remained unopened and still standing at home in the middle of our living room amidst the general clutter that accompanies the holiday season. I was amazed that it had not been opened yet.

I had considered one reason it was not opened yet was that the boys had simply received too many presents. Perhaps they were in gift receiving overload. Yes, they might have been overwhelmed. But I realized that the gifts they had received were not that many. In fact, most of what they received were clothes, games, and books. So I was even more astonished that this tall present remained unopened in the middle of our living room.

Consider first, that our hope in God can sometimes be just lying unopened right in front of us. As I thought about why the boys had not opened their present, it dawned on me that I did the same with God. Often, God has whispered something in my ear, such as *"If you start small, I will bless you in bigger ways later."* More often than not, I would not start the process God asked of me. In essence I would not open up His gift for me.

I also remembered the story of Jesus' being born in the manger. In **Luke 2:5-7**, we are told that Mary and Joseph could find no room anywhere to birth their child. The Bible specifically tells us there was no room for them in the village inn. It seemed to me this story represented a gift unopened, very similar to what I was experiencing with my boys.

The story of Joseph and Mary looking for a room mirrors the life of my boys as well as my life and yours. Consider how God presented His gift. It was placed in the womb of a virgin. She and her husband walked by faith. They came to the village inn and the gift was presented to the innkeeper.

The innkeeper looked at the circumstances around him and explained that there were no rooms available at the Inn. He was on center stage. He had choices available to him, and he chose to leave God's gift unopened. In fact, he gave the gift away.

In your life and mine, we can do the same things. God gives us an opportunity to walk by faith, and we choose to walk by sight. We can have a servant's heart or a selfish spirit. We can receive God's blessings or gifts freely, or refuse to even acknowledge the giver behind the gifts. Then we see, in our lives and the lives of those we love, that by missing God's blessing and opportunities, we can become angry, frustrated, apathetic and worse.

The innkeeper had one last chance to open a gift God had brought to his doorstep. Rolling through his mind at some point had to be the following thought. "Although there are no rooms available in the inn, I do have a room and bed myself. I could allow this very pregnant woman and husband the comfort of my room as she potentially bears this child. I could share something I have with someone who needs what I have."

Alas, the innkeeper sent Mary and Joseph on their way. He missed the amazing miracle of Baby Jesus being born that day. He could have witnessed the Creator Himself making his debut on earth. Imagine how blessed the innkeeper could have, would have, should have been. Alas, the innkeeper sent Mary and Joseph away to the stable.

OUR FAITH INCREASED

Notice that our faith can't be rewarded and increased if it is sitting unopened right in front of us. Cade and Cana, my six- and three-year-old sons, were doing the same thing. In the middle of our living room next to the Christmas tree, which was quickly losing its needles, and next to opened up packages of clothes, toys, books, and such, stood this four-foot-tall, unopened gift. I passed by it three or four times a day, and each time I was amazed. I knew if they opened it, they would be blessed. Yet, there it sat unopened.

This gift was actually the gift the boys had chosen to be opened on Christmas Eve. We were eating popcorn, sitting next to a log fire, with steamy hot cocoa. The boys chose to open this gift. It was their choice.

So the boys tore off the wrapping paper, and after looking at the picture on the box they went about roughhousing and such. The next day I asked the boys how they liked their new gift. "Well, Dad, we haven't opened it yet," Cade replied. In time as Christmas day went on, the tall gift became surrounded and squeezed out by other gifts, surprises, and activities. The gift box remained unopened.

A LIVING GOSPEL

"Wow!" I thought, as I pondered the innkeeper missing God's blessing even though the gift came wrapped in human need. Amazed, I tried to figure out the mindset of a six- and three-year-old (a futile task) that would choose to unwrap the tallest present, yet not open up the box. It was a bewildering few days to say the least. Then I sensed God was speaking to me through the situation. Here is what I learned.

First, God will surprise us with opportunities to live, grow, and be blessed by faith. We should take advantage of these opportunities. God often disguises opportunity as pain, suffering, need, and hopelessness. We can choose by faith to be blessed when all seems lost or unclear.

Second, God will sometimes wrap His *best* for us in the package of something *good*. It is up to us to choose by faith to receive His gifts even if they don't always seem like much. When we open His gifts, we are astonished at His ability to do *"exceedingly abundantly above all that we ask or think." **Ephesians 3:20*** God loves to surprise us; we just need to let Him do it. Let's open the box.

Finally, when God gives us a gift, He will eventually ask us, "How did you like your gift?" It would be most disappointing if our answer turned out to be, "I never opened it." It could be that God does not entrust us with such a wonderful gift again. We must be good stewards of His gifts or talents. The Bible states that we must take and multiply the talents or gifts that God gives us. In the end, Cade and Cana, like the innkeeper, missed God's gift. The outside of the box they unwrapped showed a picture of lawn chairs. Neither boy was interested in lawn chairs. Inside, however, there was a new tricycle for Cana, a new scooter for Cade, and enough candy to keep them fed for three months. Alas, the boys left the gift unopened. An unopened gift from God awaits your attention. Have you identified it?

Please don't leave it unopened. The biggest blessing is the sharing of all God has done in our lives after we have opened all He has put in front of us. Trust God. Choose to have a living testimony of faith full of opened blessings. Remember, unopened blessings are a testimony too.

I pray you and I will recognize God's gifts in whatever form they take and choose by faith to open those gifts by serving others, sacrificing our own ideas of how things should be, and trusting that God's *best* is better than what we believe is *good*.

Here are the three outcomes of faith:
1. *Our hope is fulfilled in God.*
2. *Our faith is increased by God through His Word.*
3. *Our life becomes a testimony or "gospel" for God's glory.*

THE FEARFUL WARRIOR

"I'm waiting!" Finally, somewhat exasperated, I groaned to God these words: "I'm waiting over here!" I had prayed, fasted, repented, read His word, scoured devotionals, sat still (hated it), sought Godly counsel and still, I'm waiting. Anybody else been there, done that? Here is an insight I pray might encourage you in God's waiting room.

Do you know someone is praying for you right now? That's right. Someone far away, or perhaps right next door, is praying for the gifts and skills God has equipped you with. You see, the need in their ministry is clear. The people are beseeching God to bring someone to help. You are that someone. They are waiting for you to hear God's call, to go and minister your gifts to their need. In some cases your spouse may be ready to marry but you are not. It may be that your lack of faith is causing the wait in your life. Let's look at Gideon's faith walk. All three outcomes of faith are related in this simple story of Gideon.

Judges chapters *6* and *7* says, *"And it came to pass, when the children of Israel cried out to the Lord because of the Midianites, that the Lord sent a prophet to the children of Israel."* This prophet reminded Israel of God's faithfulness and their own disobedience. Next, God sent an angel to the man chosen of God to minister to the needs of the children of Israel. The first words to God's chosen man, Gideon, were words of encouragement. *"The Lord is with you, you mighty man of valor."* *Judges 6:12*

The angel found Gideon threshing *". . .wheat in the winepress in order to hide it from the Midianites."* *Judges 6:11* Gideon was in a time of withdrawal. He was not exercising his highest giftedness for God's glory. In fact, he was hiding from God's call and life's great adventure. What was oppressive was expected. Fear was his constant tormentor. What he had experienced as numbness seemed normal.

God's call is never fearful, oppressive, bland, boring, or discouraging. Gideon had his focus on his circumstances, not on his God. His glance (*bleppo*) was on God and his gaze (*skopio*) was on his circumstances. Anytime we glance at God and gaze at the world, we are in trouble. Our entire focus must be a continual gaze at God and His will. Then as we glance briefly at life's circumstances, we will get clarity of vision and victory in action through prayer and God's word.

Gideon was so focused on his immediate circumstances that as God was calling him, Gideon's waiting was a function of his wavering. First, he asked the angel *"If the Lord is with us why then has all this happened to us? And where are all His miracles which our fathers told us about . . .?" **Judges 6:13** Gideon didn't realize that he, like you or me, was about to be used by God as a living miracle. Sometimes our gaze limits our vision. God or circumstances? Which do you choose to focus on?

Gideon complained that *"My clan is the weakest in Manasseh, and I am the least in my father's house." **Judges 6:15** When God calls us, we need to keep our eyes on the ball. We need to remember to separate ourselves from the things that separate us from God. These things include family, friends, expectations, traditions, and the like. We need to be ready to do things God's way and to be obedient to God's word. Finally, don't forget what God has done and is doing in our lives.

God's *". . .gifts and the calling of God are irrevocable." **Romans 11-29** What we choose to do with our gifts and calling is exactly that, a choice. God told Gideon *". . .surely I will be with you and you shall defeat the Midianites as one man." **Judges 6:16** That promise is for us today too. Will we choose to believe God at His word? Gideon didn't. His response was that if God were serious, *". . .then [He would] show me a sign." **Judges 6:17** Later, *"Gideon said to God, 'If you will save Israel by my hand as you have said, look I shall put a fleece on the threshing floor; if there is dew on the fleece only, and it is dry on all the ground, then I shall know that you will save Israel by my hand, as you have said.'" **Judges 6:36-37**

The Israelites were waiting for Gideon. Likewise people are waiting for you and me as we wait on God for an answer. He may already have given us the answer. Sometimes we wait because our faith is weak. We think "What if I obey and things don't work out?" Other times we doubt we are hearing God. God's voice never condemns, though the Holy Spirit does convict. God's voice does not discourage, though He does challenge. God's voice brings expectancy, not anxiety. Gideon, after all this waiting, still had to reverse his fleece test one more time to get it absolutely clear in his mind that it was indeed a call of God. All the while, people were praying and waiting for God to deliver them by a miracle. Gideon and his army were that miracle. God uses people just like you and me and Gideon.

Gideon finally answered the call. For him, the waiting must have been extreme. Think about it for a moment. His people are in bondage; God calls him to save the people. At some point he realizes he really is God's man. A crisis of belief ensues; he can obey or disobey. It is a scary thought because after saying "yes" to God, the next question is how to fulfill God's call.

Imagine for a moment, in a situation comparable to Gideon's, that God is calling us to begin a building project. We finally agree to lead the enterprise. Right away we assess the situation and find we have $320,000. We need ten times that amount, but we have a good start, sort of. Then, you see, God tells us to give $220,000 back to donors if they don't want to stay with the project (and they don't). In addition, God says, just as we are set to begin building, that we are allowed only $3,000 to begin. The other $97,000 is to be given away. Like Gideon, we certainly need to be humble and alert.

Immediately, we discover *"God's way is not your way, nor are His thoughts your thoughts." Isaiah 55:8* Through all of this Gideon is waiting. The Israelites are waiting as they cry to God for deliverance. The 300 chosen soldiers in Gideon's army are waiting as God forms their team. No question but that doubt, fear, frustration, perhaps division and discord, entered in as God set the stage in Gideon's call for a God-sized miracle. The whole plan is counterintuitive to our natural way of doing things.

Gideon hears a dream and interpretation, an example of God using the gifts in the body to edify one another. He divides his troops, giving every man a clay pitcher with a torch inside. Next, Gideon models a valuable lesson in leadership. *"And he said to them 'look at me and do likewise; watch, and when I come to the edge of the camp you shall do as I do.'"* **Judges 8:17** God has asked Gideon to do the improbable in the midst of the impossible—to lead a small army against overwhelming odds.

Gideon's army used clay pots to confuse and surprise the Midianites. In that day the clay pots were often used to hold the most precious possessions. The pots held valuables so robbers wouldn't be suspicious. The torches or lights in the clay pots are like our lives, a symbol of the Holy Spirit in us. We are made of clay, broken and cracked to show the light of Christ's victory. Much like jewelers who use the blackest fabric as background to highlight the most expensive diamond, God uses you and me to reveal His glory to a lost and dying world today. It may be time for you and me to come out of withdrawal. Jesus is either Lord of all or not Lord at all.

The pitchers were broken, torches raised, trumpets blown; the Midianites were devastated and captured. The power of God through Gideon's faith overwhelmed the Midianites. As Gideon was faithful, the fullness of God's supernatural power and wisdom was unleashed through Gideon's army on behalf of the Israelites. The long wait was finally over. In the same way He called Gideon, God has called you and me to a faith walk. By exercising our faith in accordance with God's will, we will experience miracles, that is, supernatural happenings. Remember, ". . .the Lord is with you, you mighty man of valor! **Judges 6:12**

BEYOND THE OBVIOUS

Consider that people and situations are not always what they seem. Pray for discernment. Seek wisdom. Give people the benefit of the doubt. Forgive easily. Risk often. The following story from my friend Bob Johnson speaks to the benefit of being a person who looks beyond the obvious.

A wealthy man and his son loved to collect rare works of art. They had everything in their collection, from Picasso to Rafael. They would often sit together and admire the great works of art.

When the Vietnam conflict broke out, the son went to war. He was very courageous and died in battle while rescuing another soldier.

The father was notified and grieved deeply for his only son. About a month later, just before Christmas, there was a knock at the door. A young man stood at the door with a large package in his hands. He said, "Sir, you don't know me, but I am the soldier for whom your son gave his life. He saved many lives that day, and he was carrying me to safety when a bullet struck him in the heart and he died instantly. He often talked about you and your love for art." The young man held out his package. "I know this isn't much. I'm not really a great artist, but I think your son would have wanted you to have this."

The father opened the package. It was a portrait of his son, painted by the young man. He stared in awe at the way the soldier had captured the personality of his son in the painting. The father was so drawn to the eyes that his own eyes welled up with tears.

He thanked the young man and offered to pay for the picture. "Oh, no sir, I could never repay what your son did for me. It's a gift."

The father hung the portrait over his mantle. Every time visitors came to his home he took them to see the portrait of his son before he showed them any of the other great works he had collected.

The man died a few months later. There was to be a great auction of his paintings. Many influential people gathered, excited over seeing the great paintings and having an opportunity to purchase one for their collections.

On the platform sat the painting of the son. The auctioneer pounded his gavel. "We will start the bidding with this picture of the son. Who will bid for this picture?"

There was silence. Then a voice in the back of the room shouted. "We want to see the famous paintings. Skip this one."

But the auctioneer persisted. "Will someone bid for this painting? Who will start the bidding? $100? $200?"

Another voice shouted angrily. "We didn't come to see this painting. We came to see the Van Goghs, the Rembrandts. Get on with the real bids!"

But still the auctioneer continued. "The son! The son! Who'll take the son?"

Finally, a voice came from the very back of the room. It was the long-time gardener of the man and his son. "I'll give $10 for the painting." Being a poor man, it was all he could afford.

"We have $10; who will bid $20?"

"Give it to him for $10. Let's see the masters."

"$10 is the bid; won't someone bid $20?"

The crowd was becoming angry. They didn't want the picture of the son. They wanted the more worthy investments for their collections.

The auctioneer pounded the gavel. "I'm sorry, the auction is over."

"What about the paintings?"

"I am sorry. When I was called to conduct this auction, I was told of a secret stipulation in the will. I was not allowed to reveal that stipulation until this time. Only the painting of the son would be auctioned. Whoever bought that painting would inherit the entire estate, including the paintings. ***The man who took the son gets everything!"***

God sent His only son 2,000 years ago to die on a cruel cross. Much like the auctioneer, His message today is "The Son, the Son, who'll take the Son?"

Because, you see, whoever takes the Son gets everything.

Agape Papa

Wow! She thought. She had covered so much in such a short time. She wanted to apply all she was learning. Suddenly, her attention was turned from the journal to something lingering in the air.

Gently, slowly, with imperceptible clarity the air became alive with a warm delightful series of odors. The fragrant and sweet smell of vegetables steamed in butter and spices pierced her olfactory glands like a sweet peach to a hungry traveler. The smell of oven-roasted turkey knifed itself through the wedged floorboards as though baked in a fresh dough-like cloud. The tinkling of glasses and silverware coupled with the occasional thud of a dish placed on the hard cherry-wood finish of the dining room table completed the melody of smells and sounds that signaled dinner was soon upon her.

Muffled voices seemed to call to her from below. There was no time to waste she thought. Life was a lot like her time in the attic. Truth is all around us, and most of us never allow our curiosity enough room to lead us to the treasure buried right in front of our noses.

She didn't want to be sleep-walking through life anymore.   She realized now that it is time to dream big! She would uncover the three mystical truths of faith in her grandfather's final journal chapter.

FAITH FACTOR NINE

Faith Factor Nine reminds us that life can be "A Gift Unopened." Faith Factor Nine notes that the three outcomes of faith are these: our hope is fulfilled, our faith is increased, and our lives become a living testimony or "gospel" for God's glory.

FAITH FACTOR NINE IN ACTION

Each one of us is a gift unopened. We all need to be opened by God and others. Can you identify your unopened gift? Do you have the courage or faith to open it now?

Note: Jesus tells us in **Matthew 7:11** *"If you then, being evil, know how to give good gifts to your children, how much more will your father who is in heaven give good things to those who ask Him!"*

Shortly after Christmas, the boys and I opened the gift. Since it was the only gift opened at the time, the boys were especially thrilled, and my heart warmed too. If I, a sinful man, would do that for my boys, consider how much more our holy heavenly Father wants to do for you. In spite of our unopened gifts, God loves you and me. That is important to remember as we give ourselves a break by faith and stop condemning ourselves for the missed opportunities or unopened gifts in our lives. Forget the past and start opening!

FAITH FACTOR TEN

Dream Big!
Three Mystical Truths of Faith

Dearest beloved,

In the end, the key is to have childlike faith.

*"Assuredly, I say to you, whoever does not receive the kingdom of God as a little child will by no means enter it." **Mark 10:15***

GOD IS WITH YOU ALL THE WAY

The first mystical truth of faith is that **God is with you all the way**. One morning, my wife and I took our two sons to La Jolla Cove in San Diego to roller-skate and ride bikes. Our six-year-old, Cade, was learning to skate. Cana, our three-year-old, was beginning to master his red tricycle. My wife and I were enjoying the beauty of the ocean and loving the time together as a family.

It soon became apparent that without proper supervision both of our boys would momentarily be in great pain. They were both enthusiastically and independently heading for disaster. Cade was quickly skate-falling toward the street and oncoming traffic. Cana was a missile, locked, loaded, and aimed at the shins and knees of unsuspecting pedestrian traffic. My wife and I immediately and intuitively split up to secure our boys and protect the general population that was currently under attack.

I ended up with Cade. When I arrived at his side, he was sprawled out on the pavement. He looked like a set of keys dropped on cement. His helmet and strap were in a "Z" shape. His arms and legs resembled a spider. Likewise, his wrist and knee guards were strewn around him in a pinwheel. He was crying.

I thought of lifting him up, but as I started to, he cried, "Don't, Daddy!" I backed off and just sat near him as he tried to collect himself. Sitting next to him, I thought of God, my heavenly father, watching me struggle to learn new things. How often I have said to Him, "Don't, Daddy!" as He has tried to help me through a difficult, painful, or challenging situation.

In my heart, I wanted to help Cade. I loved him. I wanted the best for him. God feels the same way toward me. God feels the same about you, too.

In time, Cade got up. He wobbled, bobbled, fell, and got up again. Trouble was, he didn't go anywhere. I noticed he was putting enormous effort into just standing up.

I thought about my relationship with God. I sensed I spent a lot of personal time and energy trying to stand up on my own. My heavenly father was waiting patiently at my side. He probably grimaced and shuddered with my missteps as I did watching Cade. What a waste of energy, I thought.

After much time and many bruises, I asked Cade if he wanted me to hold his arms as he learned to move forward on his skates. Since he was exhausted and frustrated, he said he did. To Cade, I was his last resort. To me, I recalled how often I waited until all my options were exhausted before calling on God. How sad.

Cade and I began to roll! He put one skate in front of the other and we moved. When he would slip on his skates, instead of falling on his face or rear, he would simply slip an inch or two into my strong, reliable arms. Smiles replaced tears. Joy broke through frustration. Hope overflowed fear. Life was grand!

That is, until he started feeling comfortable. After an hour of my supporting Cade in his skating endeavors, he actually began to move slowly on his own. So, naturally, I heard the following words: "Daddy, let go; I can do it all myself." I sensed trouble up ahead.

Like Cade, I too have said to God in so many words, "Daddy, let go; I can do it all by myself." I noticed I said it most when I became self-sufficient and overconfident in things that once required complete reliance on my heavenly father. Asking God to let go is a fatal mistake most Christians make more than once.

Cade fell hard. Tears, screams, blood on his knee, and more screams followed. I cleaned up his wound. I bandaged his cut. I thought about the many times God had to heal me from my self-inflicted traumas. I wanted to tell Cade to let me help him so that he could grow faster in his ability to skate safely.

Cade asked me through tear-soaked eyes to, "Please hold me by my shirt for a long time as I skate this time, Daddy." Wow, I thought. My six-year-old son is starting to learn spiritual lessons through his learning to skate. More accurately, my son was teaching me about God's love for me. In the same way I was treating Cade, God shows His love to me by being interested in my growth and the specific details of my life.

I also learned about God's patience and His personal interest in me and in my pursuits. I experienced God's willingness to allow me to exert my free will to the point of hurting myself. Then, when asked, God gave His grace and tender mercy to help, heal, teach, and support me to do the task or assignment set before me.

Cade stood up again. Battered and bruised, he moved forward. I held him by his shirt. As he skated, he grew more confident. Since I held him by his shirt, it looked like he was a puppet. Instead of

Cade falling now, his arms and legs would simply dangle back and forth until his feet reconnected with the rhythm of the street beneath him. Laughter and hope were squealing their way down the beachfront.

Cade's faith was now tempered with reality. His childlike faith, expressed by cries of "Daddy, I can do it," was mixed with his pain of trying too much too soon without his daddy's help and protection. Cade had learned not to take into his own hands his own steps forward. He had learned to say "yes" to his daddy's offer to guide and protect him as he learned to skate.

Cade's faith was still very childlike. But with me holding him by his shirt, he became more bold. Since his falls were now nonexistent, he was willing to try new and challenging things. He skated fast, he went on the grass, he skated on the curb, he hopped a corner, and he even skated backwards. The whole time, he was guided by his daddy's faithful hand.

God wants to bless you and me the same way. He wants to introduce us to something new in our lives. He wants to protect us from fear and failure. However, He will not step in and override our cries of "Daddy, I can do it myself." He will be there to help us up, clean us off, and give us a fresh start when we fall, but He won't protect us from falling unless we ask Him to do so.

In the end, usually to our utter surprise, when we surrender to Him, supernatural things begin to happen. Like Cade, we begin to skate fast, slip but not fall, jump curbs, and more. We are filled with a reverent awe, giddy joy, and hopeful expectation of more. God's hand on our shirts helps us up as we learn His plan for our lives. We draw closer to God as we experience His faithful love.

Cade never stopped skating that day. He loved being around his daddy. He showed off for his mommy. He showed his little brother what he could do. And then something else happened.

Cade began skating down a walkway and asked me to "Let go, Daddy." Since he had learned everything I had to teach him and had practiced under my protecting hand, I let him go. Cade picked up speed. This was not the ideal place for me to let him skate on his own. He was heading straight for a steep flight of stairs.

Cade bent his knees, wobbled, lowered his behind, and flailed his arms left and right. He stuck his jaw out while his helmet slipped back on his head. His speed was now Mach 1. I was sweating profusely. His mother had noticed the episode from across the street and was now galloping like the cavalry to Cade's rescue.

The stairs awaited straight ahead. A 90° curve was his only escape from certain mayhem for his body and banishment for me by my wife. Cade turned his body. My mouth dropped. His legs made a tight arc. My wife was now running in slow motion and screaming something I'm sure was meant for me. I was too numb to hear.

Cade's head entered the turn, his arms swinging violently to support his courageous but untrained legs. His vision never left his goal—the bench just past the turn, under the Torrey Pine tree. Whoosh! Clickity, clickity, clickity. He rounded the corner, slowed to a stop, and sat down on the bench. Cade had made it.

"Daddy, look at me!" Cade exclaimed. "Mommy, I did it, I did it! I skated all by myself and I turned!" My wife was ashen. I was astonished, proud, and amazed. My wife and I looked over at Cade with Cana on his trike at our feet. I thanked God for teaching me so much about childlike faith through my son. I praised God that my wife still loved me. In the distance, as I thought about my relationship with Cade and my relationship to God, I heard Cade say, "Daddy, let's do that again."

Remember: *God is with you all the way!*

GOD SAVES THE BEST FOR LAST

The second mystical truth of faith is that **God saves the best for last**.

> *"On the third day there was a wedding in Cana of Galilee, and the mother of Jesus was there. Now both Jesus and his disciples were invited to the wedding. And when they ran out of wine, the mother of Jesus said to Him, 'They have no wine.'*
>
> *Jesus said to her, 'Woman, what does your concern have to do with me? My hour has not yet come.'*
>
> *His mother said to the servants, 'Whatever He says to you do it.'*
>
> *Now there were set there six waterpots of stone, according to the manner of purification of the Jews, containing twenty or thirty gallons apiece. Jesus said to them, 'Fill the waterpots with water.' And they filled them up to the brim. And he said to them, 'Draw some out now, and take it to the master of the feast.' And they took it. When the master of the feast had tasted the water that was made wine, and did not know where it came from (but the servants who had drawn the water knew), the master of the feast called the bridegroom. And he said to him, 'Every man at the beginning sets out the good wine, and when the guests have well drunk, then the inferior. You have kept the good wine until now!'*
>
> *This beginning of signs Jesus did in Cana of Galilee, and manifested His glory, and His disciples believed in Him.*
>
> *After this He went down to Capernaum, He, and his mother, His brothers, and His disciples; and they did not stay there many days."*
>
> ***John 2:1-12***

Jesus' mother did three things by faith. First in verse two, she saw a need. In verse four, she stated the need not just in general to any-one, but specifically to Jesus. Third, in verse five, she submitted the need. Since she was thinking of others first, speaking to Jesus second, and trusting that He would do the rest, she secured a large blessing for someone else. The guests thanked the father with the words "you have kept the good wine until now!" Remember this— for you too God saves the best for last.

However, do not ever compromise the vision God has given YOU. The blessing of the Lord on the ministry He has given each of us, and for the people He has entrusted us with, requires you and me to move forward in spite of any well meaning opposition or fierce attack around us. If for some reason you have already made the error of caving in to the pressure, be encouraged. The Bible has a fascinating side note to a story of lost vision in the midst of terrible internal attack and lack of faith.

Moses was leading the Israelites. God gave Moses specific instruc-tions. *"Then the Lord spoke to Moses, saying 'Take the rod; you and your brother Aaron gather the assembly together. Speak to the rock before their eyes, and it will yield its water; thus you shall bring water for them out of the rock, and give drink to the congre-gation and their animals.'"* **Numbers 20:7-8**

Notice the detail of God's request. Speak to the rock. Do it in front of the people. Do it with Aaron. Drink will be provided for the whole group of people and their animals.

Notice what Moses did. He spoke to the people, not the rock: *"Hear now you rebels!"* **Numbers 20:10** He did what he did in anger toward the people, and the glory for the miracle was lost in the following statement: *"Must we bring water for you out of this rock?"* **Numbers 20:10** Moses failed to do it with Aaron. Instead

Moses alone *". . .lifted his hand and struck the rock twice with his rod. . . ."* **Numbers 20:11** God was faithful to fulfill His promise regardless of the faithlessness of Moses, for we read *". . .and the congregation and their animals drank."* **Numbers 20:11**

What happens next is as horrifying as it is bemusing. *"Then the Lord spoke to Moses and Aaron, 'Because you did not believe Me, to hallow Me in the eyes of the children of Israel, therefore you shall not bring this congregation into the land which I have given them."* **Numbers 20:12** Wow! How totally disappointing and devastating! That's it Moses; one mistake and you miss the promise I have for you. Such a judgment just seemed so harsh to me for so long. Until...

> *"Now after six days Jesus took Peter, James, and John his brother, brought them up on a high mountain by themselves, and was transfigured before them. His face shone like the sun, and His clothes became as white as the light. And behold, Moses and Elijah appeared to them, talking with Him."* **Matthew 17:1-3**

We know Moses died prior to the Israelites entering the Promised Land. We know God personally buried the body of Moses. We are sad and perplexed at the swiftness of God's judgment on Moses at the rock of Meribah. End of story, right?

Not exactly. You see God has a funny way of surprising us with His grace. The story of the water is deep and complex. Here are a few insights as they pertain to vision and leadership.

Moses had a rod that probably had buds on it in the springtime. Fruit if you will. When he struck the rock, against God's direct command, he lost the fruit of his ministry, or the opportunity to enter the promised land. The rock he struck was symbolic of Jesus. Though the people were angry with Moses and doubtful of God's provision, God was not angry with them. Moses was angry, though, and misrepresented God's ultimate plan of provision for the people by his anger.

Our reactions and responses to people always point people either toward or away from Jesus. The water represents the Holy Spirit. The fact that the people and animals were given water in spite of Moses "misrepresenting" God should be a great comfort to us all. God is always faithful even when we are not.

Like you and me, Moses was probably hurt, angry, and tired. His ministry "fell" because of the very thing that was his greatest strength. He loved the people too much. He needed to allow God to love and minister to the people in their rebellion. It was never Moses' responsibility to represent God's character in the ministry on God's behalf. God was quite capable of disciplining those folks in rebellion. God had not asked Moses to handle the rebellion on His behalf.

So if Moses "blew it," what kind of hope is there for you and me? What if we "blow it?" Aren't we living in the age of grace? Yes, and thankfully, Moses tasted God's grace too. Consider the scripture *"And behold Moses and Elijah appeared to them, talking with Him." Matthew 17: 1-3* Answer the following questions, and you will have a God-sized blessing on your hands. Where did Moses and Elijah appear? When did they appear? Why did they appear?

Moses and Elijah appeared on the Mount of Transfiguration, which, according to *The New Bible Dictionary* (p.1212), was "probably Mt. Hermon, which rises to a height of 2814 miles above sea level." Mt. Hermon is a "Mountain in the Anti-Lebanon Range, and easily the highest in the neighborhood of Palestine" (p.1212). The answer to our first question is that God placed Moses and Elijah right in the Promised Land during the transfiguration. That's right, God sneaked Moses into the Promised Land after all. Whew! That's great news!

The answer to when they appeared is simple. They appeared with Jesus to herald in the age of grace. Grace is what you and I breathe each day. Moses being there with Jesus was God's way of telling us believers that when, not if, but when, we make a mistake, God will be there to surprise us with His grace and love.

Imagine how excited Moses must have been when he heard the Father say he would meet Jesus on a Mountain in the place that God had promised him so long ago. How about you and me? Do we have promises from God that we lost long ago? Get ready; God may be preparing us for a transfiguration of our thinking. He may have a resurrection of a promise that we just now recall. Rejoice!

Finally, why did they appear on the Mount with Jesus? You and I need all the help we can get. Simply seeing Jesus with Moses brings to completion the transition between the Old and New Testaments. Grace supercedes the law. Moses in the flesh could not enter the Promised Land because he represented the law. God coming as a man in Jesus offers the ultimate sacrifice of grace on our behalf, wiping away the burden of the law.

I believe it is meant as an encouragement to us as well. Attack will come. Sometimes, like Moses, we will be so ensconced in the battle that we will forget we are called to lead, not punish the people whom God has entrusted to us. Vision in Christian ministry of any kind requires a total sacrifice. Our lives must be dedicated to God. Our lives must be submitted in slavery to those we serve.

Attack will come, and when it does, it will eventually come against the vision. When that happens, surrender it all back to Him. Let Him fight for us. We are told *"The Lord will fight for you, and you shall hold your peace."* **Exodus 14:14** When you have "Gone too far," do not despair; simply remember the story of Moses on the Mount of Transfiguration with Jesus. It will do your heart good. Remember that God saves the best for last.

GOD'S REWARDS ARE ETERNAL AND INDESCRIBABLE

The third outcome of faith is that **God's rewards are eternal and indescribable**.

"Again, the kingdom of heaven is like a merchant seeking beautiful pearls, who, when he had found one pearl of great price, went and sold all that he had and bought it." **Matthew 13:45**

The merchant here is seeking beautiful pearls. He knows what he is looking for. He has invested and paid a price to pursue the great pearl. Once he finds it, he already knows what he has sacrificed and what he is willing to sacrifice to procure it. Like the merchant, you and I can be prepared to seek and receive all God has for us.

To begin this "treasure hunt," we must first separate ourselves from the things that separate us from God. Second, we must be prepared to do things God's way. Third, we must obey God and remember all He has already done in our lives.

In the prologue I mentioned I resigned my position as Executive Pastor of a large church. My family and I did this with no prospects, no back-up plan, no reserve in the gas tank so to speak. We simply did it on faith. We heard God's still small voice calling in the wilderness. In the best way we knew how, we said, "Yes, Lord, yes."

The first thing we did was separate ourselves from the things that separated us from God. The television was turned off. Our excessive eating patterns were slowly curbed. We recommitted to exercise daily. Also, we began to rectify any relationships not completely whole in Jesus. That is we had to tell people, "I'm sorry; please forgive me." We also had to tell others that we simply forgave them unconditionally.

Next, we prepared ourselves to do things God's way. Early after our announcement to leave our position, my wife had an impression from God that whatever was next for us would not require an application or resume from us. God would authorize our next appointment. Unfortunately, my lack of faith mandated we "freshen up" the resume and apply in a conventional manner to half a dozen schools just in case we needed a safety-valve option. In spite of my faithlessness in the matter, God remained faithful.

Finally, we prayed, fasted, nourished ourselves in the scriptures, and started to keep a journal to record all God was doing. In each of our lives, God's faithfulness is written for all to see. We are all living epistles. If we try, most of us could write a small book on God's blessings in our lives. It does our hearts good when we remember all that God has already done in our lives.

Well, one night in December near the end of our time in our ministry as an executive pastor, my wife had a dream. In her dream, someone had text messaged her cell phone with the words "help me!" The time was 2:37a.m.. She believed this was *Acts 2:37* where the disciples were cut quick to the heart: *"Now when they heard this, they were cut quick to the heart, and said to Peter and the rest of the apostles, men and brethren, what shall we do?"*

Thankfully, by December, we had two equally strong and compelling options. The first was to be the CEO of a young and growing company. The second was to be Headmaster of a Christian School system. I was torn and didn't have a clear sense from God what to do.

One day in late December, after a trip to the desert to pray and read God's word and worship in song, I sensed it was time to make a choice. On Sunday, I called the pastor of the church where the school was located and withdrew my name from consideration. On Monday, after a lengthy meeting in which I intended to accept the

CEO position, it became clear to me that it would not be the Lord's best for my family and me. So...

On midday Monday, where once I had had two promising offers, I now had zip...nada...zilch...nothing. I thought for sure I had really messed things up this time. Thankfully, my impending panic attack was short-circuited by God who had the pastor call me back. What happened next was supernatural.

In sharing his heart the pastor told me how like-minded he sensed we were. He said they would still love to have me come, and then he quoted *Acts 16:6-10.*

> *"Now when they had gone through Phrygia and the region of Galatia, they were forbidden by the Holy Spirit to preach the word in Asia. After they had come to Mysia, they tried to go into Bithynia, but the Spirit did not permit them. So passing by Mysia, they came down to Troas. And a vision appeared to Paul in the night. A man of Macedonia stood and pleaded with him, saying, Come over to Macedonia and help us. Now after he had seen the vision, immediately we sought to go to Macedonia, concluding that the Lord had called us to preach the gospel to them."*

Immediately, like in *Acts 2:37*, my heart was cut to the quick. I accepted the new Headmaster/Pastoral position by faith with great hope and peace.

I learned quite clearly that even I can't mess up God's plan. I experienced first hand how delightful are God's rewards which are eternal and indescribable. The reason is that the peace and joy associated with watching God be God in my life is tremendously rich, robust, and fulfilling. God may be doing a similar work in your life too. Please let me encourage you to surrender. Allow God to direct your paths. There is no good way to predict His goodness ahead of time.

God's rewards are *". . .exceedingly and abundantly beyond all we can ask or imagine."* **Ephesians 3:20**

In **Genesis 12:1** we find the key to the Faith Factor life. It is where we actually unlock, open, and push wide away, the door that allows us to experience God's amazing plan for our abundant life.

> *"Now the Lord had said to Abram:*
> *'Get out of your country,*
> *From your family*
> *And from your father's house,*
> *To a land that I will show you.*
> *I will make you a great nation;*
> *I will bless you*
> *And make your name great;*
> *And you shall be a blessing.*
> *I will bless those who bless you,*
> *And I will curse him who curses you;*
> *And in you all the families of the earth shall be blessed.'"*
>
> **Genesis 12:1**

Are you ready? Here is the eternal and indescribable special insight on faith. It is all GOD. That's right, look at the passage in Genesis 12:1 again. It begins with *"God said."* In fact God tells Abram exactly what to do (get out of your country), who specifically to leave (his family and father's house), where to go (to a land I will show you), how he is going to fare (I will make you a mighty nation), and how his family will do too (I will bless you, make your name great), why he must go (you shall be a blessing), and finally the BIG vision (all the families of the earth shall be blessed).

All Abram had to do was obey God, one step at a time. So in **Genesis 12:2** we read, *"So Abram departed as the Lord had spoken to him...."*

Agape Papa

Dinner was called. The young lady slowly, painfully got up out of her dust-infested crouch. She stopped at a half stance and steadied herself. She was dizzy, not so much from the quick rush of blood to her head as from the life change she had just encountered. She marveled at how only a few hours earlier she had been miserably contented with her life of foolish desperation.

She realized that faith is no more than listening to God speaking in our lives. It may be through our pastor, friends, worship, prayer, nature, dreams, or any host of other methods God may choose to speak to us (perhaps even a grandfather's journal). She noted that once we know He has spoken to us, the next step is really the fun part. It is obeying. When we do these two things—listen to God and obey Him right away—we begin to live what her grandfather called the Faith Factor life.

As she closed her grandfather's journal, she noticed again the words on the cover, "A good man leaves an inheritance to his children's children." **Proverbs 13:22** *It was the first time she truly understood these words in the context her grandfather meant them. His journal contained the inheritance to eternal life in the hereafter as well as the promise of a fruitful life in the here and now. Critically for her it provided just the push she needed to make the commitment to live the fullest life for Jesus she could. It's what her grandfather would have wanted all along. It is the reason he titled his journal "The Faith Factor: Unlocking God's Amazing Plan for Your abundant Life."*

FAITH FACTOR TEN

Faith Factor Ten highlights the three keys to Dream Big! They are these: God saves the best for last, God is with you and me all the way, and God's rewards are eternal and indescribable.

FAITH FACTOR ACTION ITEM

What will you commit to do by faith once you have finished this book? Write it in a letter to yourself and give it to a friend to mail to you six months from now.

FAITH FACTOR TEN IN ACTION

What are you going to do with what you have learned in *The Faith Factor*? Explain the next action item for your life. How will you continue to grow? Tell someone so he or she can pray and help you continue to grow in your own Faith Factor life.